ACRNS

ENTHRALLING STORIES FROM
~ A BOARDING SCHOOL ~

ACORNS

ENTHRALLING STORIES FROM A BOARDING SCHOOL

An Anthology
by

Pat Corbett   Vipin Sehgal   Raghu Menon   Anurag Sinha
Manoj Panikkar   Sweta Srivastava Vikram   Amit Suri
Gary Senger   Mangu Srinivas   Nitin Dubey
Kanishka Mallick   Sudip Bajpai   Vikas Chandra
Raveesh Gupta   Nikhil Kumar   Tabish Nawaz
Priyanka Pandey   Shrikant Avi   Vani Raj   Prabhat Ranjan

HTTPS://TWAGAA.COM

HTTPS://TWAGAA.COM

Mumbai (MH), India
Website: https://twagaa.com
Email: hello@twagaa.com

First published by TWAGAA INTERNATIONAL 2020
Copyright © TWAGAA INTERNATIONAL 2020
All Rights Reserved.

Title: ACORNS - *Enthralling Stories from a Boarding School*

ISBN: 978-93-90488-73-5

First Edition
Published in India

Cover Illustration - Sucharita Suri https://sucharitas.world
Cover Design - Seek Red https://seekred.com

Ordering Information:
Quantity sales: Special discounts are available on quantity purchases by corporations, associations, and others. For details, contact the publisher at the address or email above.

All disputes are subject to Mumbai jurisdiction only.

Of Childhood,
By Oakgrovians.

OAK GROVE SCHOOL

Oak Grove School is a residential public school, owned and run by the Indian Railways. It perches upon the many hills that dot the old road trek from Dehradun to Mussoorie, in a tiny stop called Jharipani. Its campus covers 256 acres (1.04 sq. km.) of beautiful hills, with playgrounds, a valley and buildings, situated amidst local flora and fauna including groves of lush oak trees and troops of inquisitive langurs.

The school was founded by the East Indian Railway Company on 1 June 1888. The students at Oak Grove are predominantly children of Indian Railways employees, with 25% of seats reserved for other children. The school has three semi-independent wings — Oak Grove Senior Boys' School (commenced 1888), Oak Grove Senior Girls' School (1897), and Oak Grove Junior School (1912). The school buildings were designed by Mr. Richard Roskell Bayne, Chief Engineer, East Indian Railway Company.

With an alumni strength of over 5000, Oakgrovians are spread across every corner of the world, bound by the common thread of a childhood spent in this salubrious, green, and wonderful environment of a Himalayan boarding school.

FOREWORD

Gentle Reader, please don't ask me what am I doing scribbling a foreword to a book - a garland of memories – by boys and girls who, in their once-upon-a-time days, all wore a maroon blazer? There are, after all, writers greater than me in the hill station where Oak Grove School happens to be. But I'm not exactly the type to look a gift-horse in the mouth. After all 'in a single acorn sleep a thousand forests.'

I was five years old when I first heard of the Railway School from my Grandfather. He had, on a lark, decided to take me on a walk down the old bridle path to Rajpur and beyond. That was the road taken by the early pioneers and empire builders, where at an elevation of 5, 500 feet above sea level, on the 1st of June 1888, the East Indian Railways had taken over and moved the school from the Nepal Ranas' Fairlawn Palace to its present location in Jharipani, straddling the first ridge of the Himalaya. Take away Oak Grove, set in an emerald isle of two hundred sixty-five acres and the stupendous view of the Doon, and there is not much left to keep the visitor here.

Near the school gate, on a bend stands a relic from the

Raj, with a curious inscription: 'Sacred to the memory of Sir C. Farrington, Bart., Captain of Her Majesty's 35th Regiment, who departed this life on the 28th March 1828, aged 35 years.'

It took several years of sleuthing to brush off the schoolboy tales of rebellious soldiers decapitating their commanding officer. He was being brought up the hill to recuperate at the Landour Convalescent Depot from burns suffered in a shipwreck, when the forefingers of death pounced upon him and the end came here.

'There is something extremely melancholic in the desolation of the spot. He had been aboard the Kent East Indiaman when she perished in a fire in the Bay of Biscay on 1st March 1825,' wrote Captain Thomas Skinner, in 1828. He laments: 'To be buried where no Christian ever lived, and none before him died.'

I owe a debt of gratitude to Patrick Corbett, who had come 'home' to attend a school reunion. It was he who gave me a rough transcript of the Principal's Diaries - a priceless record of the trials and triumphs of education in 'the Etons of the East' in the days of their infancy. You have to see the impressive calligraphy of Principal K. F. McGowan's handwriting to believe how he coolly steered the school's destiny in the choppy waters of the post-Independence years. It is these same very years that you find in this collection.

Acorns has tales of growing up in a boarding school that often leave a bitter-sweet taste in your mouth, as you find in Tabish Nawaz's The Architecture of Solitude; or Shrikant Avi aboard a train heading to school; or Gary Sengar's memoirs tell you tales of his puppy love for his teacher; and the intrepid Vipin Sehgal, now living in Canada, reminisces his class getting a day off to welcome the Dalai Lama at Kolhukhet.

Indeed tall oaks do from little acorns grow.

Happy reading!

Ganesh Saili
Mussoorie, India
December 2020

PREFACE

The anthology *ACORNS* has been compiled on an impulse, typical and true of boarding school students, whose spirit and enthusiasm often make them do more as a team than what they would do as individuals. In the book, twenty former students have shared a part of their lives in the form of stories, anecdotes, tributes, and memoirs that they had once lived as the children of the school they grew up in.

Through these stories, they show the world that the days lived at Oak Grove, though away from their family, were amazing and abundantly filled with joie de vivre. To this day, remembrances of the time at their alma-mater makes their eyes moist - sometimes with laughter, and sometimes with memories of people and places they have loved and miss dearly.

Leaf through these pages to discover true emotions, surreal experiences, enthralling anecdotes, and grateful nostalgia, from people who are the 'Children of Oak Grove'.

Amit Suri
Oakgrovian, 1995 batch

CONTENTS

UNLEARNING THE QUEEN'S ENGLISH

~ Sweta Srivastava Vikram

"You are expected to learn at least five new English words every day, memorize their meanings, and use them appropriately," announced my boarding school's single, svelte, smart, headmistress, Ms. Sharma, at the beginning of every semester. My school was spread over 250 acres of lush hills in Mussoorie, India.

We boarders, like typical teenagers, snickered at the English-loving protégé of the founding fathers. We soon caved in when words like, "You will pay a fine if caught speaking in Hindi," started echoing in the hallways.

"What else can we do? We get ten rupees as tuck money and

have an insatiable boarder's appetite," said the queen of rebellion, my classmate, Rajani. We all resisted but, in the end, pragmatism won. We couldn't risk depriving ourselves of the only gentleman we saw over the weekends—the tuck man and the array of goodies he brought, like Santa at Christmas.

The students waited expectantly for his coconut macaroons, Mango Frooti, and cream-filled rolls. I, too, went from thinking, speaking, and debating in the Queen's English to dreaming in it. I didn't want to take any chances. What if Ms. Sharma confronted me in my dreams and deprived me of the weekend decadence?

My obsessive-compulsive relationship with the English language might have begun in Mussoorie, but it didn't end at school. On one occasion, my mother yelled at me because I corrected a relative when they said, "I am having to go to the wedding." I was rebuked, "This is what you have been taught? To tell elders they are wrong!" Maybe I shouldn't have said anything, but I was beyond cure by then. Years and years of emphasis on accurate diction, pronunciation, and grammar had turned me into a grammar maniac.

In 2005, when I joined an Ivy League college in the United States for a master's program in communication, I thought, how difficult can it be? A significant number of Americans I had interacted with used grammar erroneously. A few used 'like' a little too often in their sentences. Others said, "Stand on line," blithely. When a coworker said, "Irregardless of what they say, I could have went there," I was convinced that I would sail smoothly through grad school.

In my first semester at Columbia University, I signed up for a course called Business Writing for the Media. I was the classic Indian student—sat in the first row, hand raised to answer every question, and stayed back late to confirm that I hadn't missed anything. I was trained to think that earning a 4.0 GPA was the only measure of good performance. Though I was an adult by this time, fear of performance appraisals from my childhood continued to haunt me. "96%? Where did you lose the remaining 4% marks?"

Day one in class was disastrous. Let's just say 'ungrammatical' was my professor's choice word for that evening. "You might want to read On Writing Well," he suggested. I was baffled. It was like telling Cleopatra how to rule Egypt. "The English that you speak and write would be a misfit in the American world of communication. If you want to survive, you have to relinquish the Queen's English and accept the Americanized version," he continued in a more compassionate tone.

I could not believe my ears. Saying, "Please find attached my resume for your perusal," or, "I had been waiting for the article to finish," was incorrect? When I read out one of my PR pitches in class, my classmates gave me a confused look. One sentence read, "The yoga guru looks sober." In Queen's English, sober means somber, in the United States it refers to a non-drunk person. The professor said, "It's not just the extra 'o's' and 'u's' you need to eliminate from your vocabulary (neighbor vs. neighbour); you need to get rid of passive voice, convoluted sentences, and flowery language." But I was taught that passive voice was the cultured and sophisticated style of expressing oneself. Wasn't flowery language synonymous with a good command over words? "If you can't finish reading a sentence in one breath, then you know it's too long," the professor reiterated.

It was clear I had to unlearn whatever I had learned my entire life. I came home and howled like a baby. In my Indian high school, I was the popular editor-in-chief of my school's publication. Words were what I knew best. The talent and skill set that I had been proud of my entire life was now redundant. I made a note to self, 'Tonight I went from reigning grammar queen to a lonely tuba player.'

Over a period of time and after several splashes of red ink across my assignments, I warmed up to American English. The ride from the colloquial, Indianized version of the Queen's English to the Yankee version was an interesting, bumpy experience. When my friend showed me a copy of the recommendation written by his former boss at one of the global firms in India, I instantly understood why the top schools in the United States hadn't accepted him. One recommendation went, 'I am having to say that Ravi is having a lot of good qualities.'

I wonder if a language is a matter of perspective. Who decides whether it should be tomatoes or to-mah-toes? I wonder what response my Queen's New York, English would evoke if I were to return to my school in Mussoorie today, where Queen's English continues to reign.

THE ARCHITECTURE OF SOLITUDE

~ Tabish Nawaz

(1)

For Tushar, Tuesdays and Thursdays were important days. On these days, from across the valley, Madiha visited the common Computer and Biology Labs in the Boys' School. This provided Tushar an opportunity to exchange – furtively – glances, smiles and letters with Madiha. The two days stood out as some musical minarets among the dull, raucous ruins of Tushar's dreary weekly routine. He prepared for their arrival and looked up to them, as a chance to shape his unreflecting dilapidated days into some shiny forms.

(2)

Becoming a ninth grader had given Tushar some degree of freedom, which only days ago, while he was in eighth standard, was restricted. Now, he had some leeway to make special friends living across the valley, in the Girls' School. Partially moved by his own loneliness, and also to see if Madiha would be interested in his companionship, Tushar sat one night, alone, scribbling an ornate letter to her, taking unusual care about the language, which of course was English – the daily and familiar form of his speech – but in form and appearance, as if English's rich relative – flashy, gaudy, loud. The flowery prose began by proclaiming Madiha as the sweetest person alive and wished that Tushar's letter finds her in the pink of health – the expressions that were to bring a smirk on his face, many years later.

In the letter, Tushar described seeing Madiha on the playground for the first time, while he was playing cricket with his classmates in the front pitch, and she walked toward the rest house with her parents – who were visiting her then. Tushar reflected on his sensitivity in the letter, that he was a vulnerable person, worthy of Madiha's interest. Nobody told Tushar, but it seemed he understood as to how to win over a person, that he knew it was vulnerability that made one dear to another.

Tushar narrated the brief moment of sighting Madiha, more or less the way it actually occurred. He wrote that after Madiha faded into the distance, as she descended the stairs leading to the rest house, he looked around and found that each of his classmate had magically transformed into himself. As if only he existed in every human form, all acting like him – full of desire and confused, all equally struck by Madiha's presence, swooning, wishing to be with her forever.

During the prep time in the evening, sitting next to his desk partner, Arhan, Tushar disclosed his incipient feelings for Madiha. Arhan recommended him to forget about her, as everyone in the class desired her and we didn't stand a chance. Arhan's emphasis on 'we' betrayed his inner feelings and made him sound more credible. But what riled Tushar - he wrote in the letter – that Arhan said, 'We are like crippled-men in this pursuit, and there are many other more able in the class already, who too share the same feeling'. Tushar wrote the following poem to her in the proposal.

Of Love and Crippled Men

With a movement of – a bough
- trembling, you came   to disrupt our cricket match.
We all stopped to watch you pass
before the game resumes,   a crippled man I knew,
made further by this event, couldn't move on.
I was standing nearby   so he asked
in a voice talcum soft   "Who's-that-girl?"
I looked smilingly
          "She's the one everyone loves"
              "He, he, that, that, everyone"

He looked at the far end   of the field
just to hear a name   who may not love her
asked me   "Even-that-one?"
"The one with the unkempt beard and pants high above his
heels?"
"Yes, even that one!"
He grew despondent
turned his head in the direction   where
your vestige was fading in the horizon

The first letter ended here.

The wait for Tushar was long. For weeks no response came. Many Tuesdays and Thursdays arrived and crumbled into the ruins of his routine, recognizable only with their shiny hopes in their beginnings and carbonaceous disappointments in the middles and the ends. As the days wore on, Tushar was explaining to himself the possible reasons – the letter might not have reached her, those responsible for delivering it must have misplaced it, or worse still, Madiha may be suffering from some illness and would send her reply when she regains her vigor.

By now, everyone in the class knew that Tushar had written a letter. They were convinced of his rejection, and planned to write letters themselves, seeking Madiha's friendship in return.

Until Madiha's reply came, Tushar had lost any distinction of his days – all seven felt to him like one heavy mass of stone, forever kept in his shirt's pocket, their weight felt each passing moment. Even when his shirt changed, it was somehow there, even the school washer man had made a complaint against him, about the unusual sand Tushar's shirt released upon washing, as if its fabric were made of stone. Tushar had come to realize that he would soon be buried among such stones.

All this changed, and a sapling burst forth from the stone, when Madiha's reply came. Their epistolary friendship began. The path of Tushar's weekly routine now passed through the two destinations – its Tuesday and Thursday. He now began to feel the presence of an architecture among his ruins.

(3)

It was a Tuesday. The ninth-grade girls from the Girls' School, descended into the valley, in their maroon blazers, the entourage moving so close to one another and in unison, it appeared as if a mass of cloud, dyed maroon, was brushing past the earth. The hum that usually accompanied them was missing. The landscape - though visually appealing, but due to the pervading silence - felt like it was hiding something ominous within its layers.

Not given into recognizing these finer signs, Tushar left his classroom to meet Madiha, wearing a meticulously clean and ironed uniform, soft and lush sweater, a shiny pair of shoes and exquisite perfume, most of which belonged to more than one person. He carried a letter in his shirt's pocket, written on a fancy letter pad, which contained such quotes whose pronunciation would turn the most brutish of a person into a sensitive soul.

Writing these letters was never a simple affair, it required utmost care, making it a work of craft, polished repeatedly to showcase the gentle side of the author, in as poetic a manner as possible. The content was equally matched by the ornate design of the letter pads, which were purchased on Mussoorie trips - as would a sufferer of chronic gastrointestinal ailments purchase his medicines – various and indiscriminate. The point was to write each letter on a different letter pad. Therefore, it often happened that a group of students, when purchasing the letter pads, would go together, each buying a different one, with a tacit understanding that one would share their purchases whenever needed by another. This worked and nothing acrimonious came out of this practice. What can possibly go wrong in writing letters after all?

Tushar had seen the blazing maroon from a distance, while walking to the Computer Lab. His pace was nervous, but he betrayed nothing. Tushar knew that he must appear confident with all his fake exhibitions. Without confidence all his efforts would be worth nothing but mud. Perhaps this ostentation had made him fail to see anything outside of him. Tushar was so inwardly consumed in such moments that if he smiled looking at Madiha, he actually first imagined himself smiling before her, worrying as to how he looked in those moments, and often missed Madiha's smile.

Tushar reached near the maroon mass of the students, but no one came forward, not even Madiha. In fact, he found his presence repelling them, for from whichever side he tried to approach, the girls shifted away from him. He looked for Madiha, but she was not there. The letter, now within his palm, had begun to moisten. Tushar felt someone put a hand on his shoulder. He turned to find a few teachers from the Girls' School standing behind him, while a bearer's hand gripped him firmly. Though initially flustered, he managed to wish the teachers. The bearer demanded the letter, as if he knew Tushar had one. A teacher told Tushar that all his letters have been seized from Madiha, and they were read before the Girls' School morning assembly. Tushar felt embarrassed in that moment, thinking about the time he took to embellish those letters, meant only for Madiha, for sharing his solitude with her. The bearer huddled Tushar and shoved him toward the Principal Office. While walking, the teachers gloated in triumph and tears began to roll down from Tushar's cheeks.

The landscape fast turned into a ruin, its architecture dissolving, as Tushar's feet dragged along, raising dust.

THE SIGHTING
~ *Manoj Panikkar*

Hill stations have an intimate relationship with all things paranormal. It has something to do with the mist, the creeping early darkness of the days, the covered faces of people that walk past you in the mall road, the stories of Englishmen buried in long forgotten graveyards. All of this serves as fertile ground for imagination to go on the overdrive.

At Oak Grove School, we virtually lived with these denizens of the paranormal world. Some of them had become heirlooms, passed on from one generation to the next. We knew them well, even if we did not see them. We knew how they'd appear out of the woodwork, ubiquitously, make their presence felt and then recede back to the shadows, shone just enough to keep the legends alive. So, Kanji Lal happened, rumoured to have fatally fallen down the wooden stairs in the Boys School Dormitory, Principal Watts, who shot himself, and the fabled horse borne headless rider in the Valley. There was this notorious one in Girls School and another one that regularly stopped our history teacher outside what was formerly the half-way house to ask for cigarettes. The school hospital was the den of scary apparitions, manifesting themselves in the form of dripping taps, banging doors and more.

As a teenager in the Oak Grove Boys School, I yearned for my own encounter with these phantoms. However, they decidedly eluded me for much of my 10 formative years there. It was late towards my final year in school that I decided to take matters into my own hands. It was a few weeks before our high school examination. I belonged to a group that stayed up late in the class for self-study, purely driven by peer pressure. On the day, it was snowing lightly outside. My friend, Joydeep, and I, looked out into the darkness from the class, and began a conversation, overheard and moderated by the rest of the class. How about a jaunt up at 1 a.m. to the school valley? Would that constitute sufficient cause for expulsion, should we be caught? The casual ribbing surreptitiously took the form of a careful exploration of the possibility. The glass window that protected the class from the elements was closed, but it could be opened. Once outside, we could walk out. If the *chowkidar* and his dogs do not chase us down we could walk calmly down to the valley or see the hamlet of Jharipani by the midnight. Subconsciously, I thought, we could have that much desired spectral encounter. My classmates, buried deep into their books, were amazed at the stupidity of these thoughts, but not so surprised by the direction this conversation was going.

Well, it so happened that after evaluating our options for a few minutes carefully, we pushed open the swivel windows and scampered through outside into the cold air. We were in our dressing gowns and leather shoes, nothing less than wraiths ourselves. The path that started off from our classroom through to the Boys School gate was covered by a sprinkling of snow, illuminated by lamps that gave it an eerie glow. As Joydeep and I turned from the school gate and undertook the walk that led to the Principal's residence, we positively looked like spooky, albeit shabby versions of the more seasoned ghosts of Oak Grove. The moonlight gave us little room to hide. We walked grimly by the edge of the road, so that if someone called out, we could jump over the *pushta* and disappear into the shadows. But on that night, as on, I am sure most other nights, there was not a soul in sight. We walked down to the Principal's residence, steered ourselves towards the steep incline towards the valley, past the inscription that said "Work is thy duty, reward is not thy concern". The wind turned into a howl during the descent, creating the perfect environment for our reckoning. It cut through our dressing gowns and the layers underneath as we took that final turn to behold our glorious valley green by the night.

The sight that unfolded before our eyes took our breath away. We pushed the Valley gate open, and watched the immense spread of white, flecks of snow, glimmering in the moonlight. The cast was all the same, but it was as if they were dressed up for an act that had an invisible audience. The old mountain behind the valley, that ever-present sentinel, reared like an old man with unkempt silver stubble. The tracks that circumambulated the valley echoed with whispered glories as they disappeared into the mist. The pavilion shrouded in mystery as if it were protecting a past. The Valley seemed to stretch out to eternity, with the little sheds at the far end, barely visible. If ever there was a perfect setting for a revenant, this was it. We stood there stunned, our breath mingling with the mist, as we stared at the sight that surrounded us. We stood there, just two awkwardly dressed boys, ill suited and encroaching, upon this play of lights, this dance of the shadow, this overwhelming opera of the senses. We saw the mist rise, take a shape, a form, an equine, a rider? In that moment unreal, we tried to see things that we wanted to see. We could always laugh silly about it after, but we were serious about it then. The cold wafted biting into our bones, as we realised, that we had to head back. The last forlorn look back at the valley, shone it as always, at its best, poised for another day, another promise.

On the way back, we took multiple stops. We walked easier, with little purpose, as it seemed like the night belonged to us. There was no one else around us, at that time of the night, who could own the sights, other than the narrow drizzle of snow and the whispering spirits that inveigled our senses. We were just another pack that saw this night at Oak Grove and like so many others we will remember this night and take this experience to dinner place conversations and reunions. The spirits that we had seen, the conversations that we have had with them. And yet, there was something that we had left behind that night at the valley. Something that we did not take down to the plains, to our upcoming struggles. Something that will merge with the folklore of Oak Grove and become a silent audience on such moonlit nights for an eternity. In the end it was a rather uneventful night.

Joydeep was inscrutably humming an old Hindi hit "Rahen na Rahen hum..." just as we ducked back into our now empty classroom. I looked up the time on my watch. It was 3 a.m.[1]

◆

---

1. *3 a.m. is referred in folklore as the witching hour or devil's hour, i.e. a time of night associated with supernatural events.*

FIRST LOVE
~ *Gary Senger*

In mid-1993, India had only 25 states. The demand for a separate state of Uttaranchal was on the rise. Throughout the proposed state of Uttaranchal, there were disturbances with frequent processions, lock-ups, and *bandhs*, adversely disrupting the civil life of citizens. The daily routine of the Queen of Hills, the other name of Mussoorie, was in disarray.

Mussoorie, incidentally, also boasts of some of the best residential schools in India. During those troubled days when history was being made, I was studying as a boarder in one of the good schools where I witnessed these historic events that now seem so distant.

That summer, we were returning from vacations. The class tenth board exam results were better than expected. We regaled in our achievements, fully consumed with our well-earned academic superiority. Young we were, and the demand for smaller independent states did not occupy any importance in our head.

My school was located in one corner of Mussoorie. It is a fully residential school. We were somewhat cut-off from the main area and were not always disturbed by the events in Mussoorie. In fact, the senior boys were enjoying it, since most of the teachers had gone on leave to shift their families to places they felt were safer and more secure. The students, therefore, had entire days at their disposal to spend at will.

Against this backdrop, the school administration came up with arrangements to make up for the academic loss. "Senior boys and girls will have joint classes on a temporary basis. As soon as the shortage of teachers ends, so would the arrangement." Under normal conditions, the school has separate a setup for Senior Boys and Senior Girls. Except for the Principal's office, the two schools had the whole infrastructure set independently with no resource shared with each other.

The boys were overjoyed with the announcement. I cannot comment about the girls, but I believe the feelings must have been the same. Maybe the new concept would provide logistical benefits, and going forward, pave the minds towards a co-education system.

The boys craved for the new guests in the class scheduled for the coming week. Among the teachers who were to come to Boys' School to teach was the Physics teacher, Miss Tanya Banerjee. She was a good-looking lady in her early twenties, who had graduated from college recently and was a Civil Services aspirant. The memory of Miss Tanya entering our classroom on the very first day lingers fresh in the mind like a sweet dream. She had sharp features with big beautiful eyes, which made her look innocent and energetic. Her perfect hourglass figure swayed as she walked. Her curly hair fell graciously and bounced on her lithe shoulders. The whole class was enchanted with her magic when she introduced herself in that lilting voice as if an air hostess was welcoming the passengers on board on a flight to heaven. I wondered why she took to teaching when she looked better than most models of those times. I was so spellbound by her beauty that her class sessions would pass in admiring her. The way she moved her hands, crushed the chalk between her long fingers, pushed her hair behind with the back of her hand, and picked the duster made most of us go weak in the knees. Her fascinating smile, while she talked, would make it but necessary to look only at her delicate lips. Every action of hers was full of grace, every move of hers was royal - her presence was magical - as if she was a magician hypnotizing the audience.

With Miss Tanya around, the environment of the school changed for the better. The boys of yesterday became the gentlemen they should be. Be it their etiquette or their getup, everything that would make Miss Tanya look at them, was worked on by the boys. The washerman was now often scolded for not paying enough attention to ironing. The tailor and the barber were unusually busy, driven by the boys for results beyond the best of their abilities. No senior boy would take slackness in appearance and mannerism. Many out-of-the-world stunts were enacted to be 'Mr. Perfect' in order to impress the fairest in the fairer sex. The boys even volunteered for jobs they would shun earlier. One such job was to get the classroom ready for lectures - check everything to be in place, all tube lights lit, blackboard clean, apparatus working, chalk, duster, charts, etc. to be set neatly in order. The truth was that the first boy, the cleanest, was also the first person to greet the girls to their seats under the new arrangement. The work of cleanliness became a matter of pride. Among the boys, a schedule was decided so that everybody got a fair chance with the fair ones. The discipline of the boys hostel improved beyond the warden's expectations. The school administration was visibly pleased by the transformation.

The concept of coexistence in coeducation extended to the games period too. The Girls Physical Training Instructor (PTI) supervised the athletic preparation for the coming meet. The school seemingly was having a big carnival.

After a few classes by Miss Tanya, we began to understand her better. Under the fair soft exterior, she had an iron heart. Some boys were caught unawares in the trap of discipline she had laid. Anybody who dared to take advantage of this good looking femme-fatale had to eat a humble pie, be it in class or anywhere else. She did not hesitate to take action against the senior boys either. Strangely, when acts of indiscipline were reported to the headmaster, we noticed a changed man in him for any complaint relating to Miss Tanya. The relaxed students, who would be given passing marks earlier out of sheer pity, had a tough time making the grades in Physics. On the timetable on the wall of the classroom, the 'Physics' periods were marked in black. Studies were a serious affair, so believed Miss Tanya, and she never accepted slackness. All the homework given by her was checked and corrected on time. So the assignments had to be completed without delay because no excuse was entertained. The defaulters were made to stand in awkward muscle-straining positions in her classes. Delicate flowers amongst us now started to turn pale, every time they heard the word 'Physics'.

Despite her terrorising methods, Miss Tanya was still a star among the boys. She was nicknamed 'sweet poison', despite all the hullabaloo of her toughness, we admired her for her beauty. Most of our free time was consumed in discussing 'sweet poison'. The grapevine was that she had participated in the Miss India contest and had won the swimsuit round. This rumour was soon found to be false but many boys continued to believe that she had indeed won the contest.

While the minds of the boys in the school were consumed, either directly or indirectly, by the physics teacher, the demand for Uttaranchal was gaining momentum. Government employees all over Uttaranchal were on indefinite strike and it was expected that the staff of the schools of Mussoorie and Dehradun should follow suit and close the school. The local protesting unions drafted a routine, which was forwarded by the teachers association to our school administration. The sermon required every school to take out a procession on the Mall road of Mussoorie on the day allotted to the school. We were overjoyed to hear that there would be no teaching on these few days.

Our joy was short-lived. The school authority decided to station more sentries at the main gate. The main gate of our school was around two kilometers from the building where classes were held. On the way, any visitor would have to pass through the Junior School which housed students till class five. It was thought that before activists could reach the main building, the information would be conveyed by the sentries faster on the telephone to the school administration, providing us enough time to call off the classes and assemble the students in the dorm. The game of 'hide and seek' continued for almost a month, until we got a chance to go to the town, where the matter of school conducting the classes clandestinely was brought to the notice of the Youth Brigade of the protesters. They promised action and we were happy to comply with it, in the hope that we will get more time to play than to be in the classrooms.

The next day, our Principal was warned tersely to bear the consequences if the school took the movement lightly. Therefore, to be safe, a date was announced for the yearly exams, after which the school would be closed for a long vacation until normalcy resumed in the hills. This meant extra classes were needed to be conducted to expedite the completion of the syllabus. The boys did not mind studying till late at night in the dormitory, because the school management believed that only dorms were a safe haven where classes could be conducted without drawing attention.

The idea of Miss Tanya teaching us in the informal environment of the dorm, while we were in our pajamas, opened doors to newer imaginations. When Miss Tanya used to come, the boys were at their best, neatly dressed in their gowns, hair combed, teeth shining, wishing her good evening and good night politely; but Miss Tanya remained terse as ever to keep her students under control.

The movement in the town had turned violent on many

occasions. One day, events took such a turn. The school, which was to take out the procession, had only girl students, with more foreigners than Indians. Like all other schools, who had demonstrated before them, they were to gather at one end of Mussoorie by 11 o'clock. From there they would go ahead with the local lady activists. The day was bright, the sun was shining just over the hills on the east, when the locals started gathering at the designated place much before the girls arrived. The crowd swelled much more than the area could accommodate. By 10 o'clock, the crowd was large enough to create problems for the police. The administration ordered for more force from the District Headquarters, if any untoward incident were to occur. The additional security force was still on the way when a miscreant in the crowd lobbed a stone at the police. Fearing trouble, the police fired a few shots at the crowd, injuring a few and hurting one critically. A curfew was imposed immediately in the town. The hill town, with limited access points into and out of the hills, now had the logistics disrupted badly, making the lives of the public and the residential schools difficult. Food supplies were hard to get hold of and this shortage made things miserable. The fear of similar untoward protests convinced the authorities to order the closure of all schools in the next fifteen days.

Our school administration started preparing for Half Yearly examinations. The examination schedule was adjusted in such a way that we could go home after a fortnight. To be honest, the examinations were a mere formality now. Arrangements were made all around the school's premises - auditorium, indoor sports halls, dining hall, etc. That is, any place where space was available for conducting exams for all classes simultaneously in the least number of days. The teachers were more than willing to help children clear their examinations. A remarkable change was observed in Miss Tanya too. She helped us with the Physics paper, obliging everyone with probable questions for the exams. The countdown to go home was the only thing on everyone's mind. The charmed boys though had additional things on their minds - thanks to Miss 'Sweet Poison'. There were rumours that the local administration had refused to provide security to run the schools. They didn't have the force in sufficient numbers to provide security to each and every organisation. The examination was somehow over in the next two weeks, and the following day we all were leaving for our homes.

That day, in the afternoon after lunch, I was playing tennis with my classmates. The tennis courts were located a little away from the main school building. They were in a natural depression in the hill, just below the auditorium building, and in the extension of the football ground. At the corner of the same ground, adjacent to the tennis courts, was the squash court. The viewer gallery of the squash court was a verandah with comfortable chairs for the audience. The verandah overlooked the tennis courts, the football field, and the Doon valley further away. A stair led to these courts from the main road via the auditorium main gate. The other end of the football field had a gate, which opened to the residences of the Principal and teachers. The same road also led to the Girls' School and Junior School.

We were enjoying our game of tennis, while some other boys were engaged in football. The weather was pleasant. It was the monsoon season when the Himalayas are rather unpredictable - within a few minutes, a sunny day could be transformed into a torrential downpour. It would take a fraction of a moment for the weather to turn ugly, bringing outdoor activities to a halt. There was a local saying which went: when the going is smooth, the rain god prefers to dance. That is exactly what happened that day too; the sun switched off and a heavy downpour started suddenly. I ran for cover and kept my belongings in the squash court, while all of my classmates ran back to the hostel building. While I fumbled with the lock on the door of the squash court, I was fully drenched. The rain was so heavy that the stairways had turned into a stream flowing with full zeal. I decided it was better to wait for the rain to subside.

While I waited there, around fifteen minutes later, Miss Tanya appeared on the far end of the football field entering from the gate facing the Principal's compound. I do not know why but I felt anxious, turning pale, as if by staying there in the squash court, I had committed a grave act of indiscipline. Though Miss Tanya was of helpful nature, only a naive one would undermine the bewitching terror she could be as 'sweet poison'. For a moment I thought she wouldn't recognize me from that distance. I collected my stuff and walked outside. All the enthusiasm I had gathered to run away came crashing the moment I saw the force of water flowing down the stairs. I consoled myself and decided to face the consequence. I knew in my heart and mind that there was nothing I had done wrong, but we boarders are trained to think that anything out of line is an act of indiscipline. While I dilly-dallied in a state of indecision, Miss Tanya walked inside the squash court. She was drenched from top to toe, water dripping from her body and clothes. A small pool soon formed where she stood. I, a good student and a thorough gentleman, wished her "Good Evening, Ma'am", modulating my tone and body gesture to be cautiously polite and sweet. She nodded, "Good Evening! But what are you doing here all alone?", she asked in her usual soft tone that had deceived us so many times earlier.

I replied that I had come to lock the door of the court when it started to rain heavily. Therefore, in order to avoid getting drenched, I stayed there and have been waiting since. I was trying to find a genuine explanation and said all this in a hurry. She didn't comment on my explanation and avoided eye contact by gazing at the electrical fittings on the ceiling of the squash court. This also gave me the chance, and courage, to look at her directly. She was wearing a blue *saree*, probably of silk, with a matching turquoise sleeveless blouse. Her wet hair was resting on her shoulders, the water still dripping from it. She had started to shiver as the evening and the rain colluded to make the weather cold. I could see that she was moving her toes to fight the numbness that typically sets in when the body loses heat.

"Ma'am, you are completely wet," I said offering my fresh hand towel to Miss Tanya. The towel was not big enough but was good enough to help her in that awkward situation. She didn't refuse, "Yes, I forgot my umbrella in Girls' School!". Her reply made me comfortable. She wiped her hair with my small towel. The wet saree had clung to her body, revealing her fair skin. She looked sensuous. Having wiped her hair and face, she bent down to dry her feet. She took off her sandals and started to wipe her toes. I tried my best to look in the other direction but just couldn't, despite my strong will. I kept admiring her beauty voyeuristically. The *pallu* of her saree slipped a little exposing a portion of her shoulders and bosom. To my utter surprise, she did not try to cover herself! "Was she ignorant, or was there more to it?", I wondered. I was awestruck. A moment later, she got up, threw the saree pallu back, and stretched her arm toward me to return the towel. "Thank you!", she said softly with a bewildering smile, squeezing my hand as she passed the towel to me.

My hormones were now ruling my mind. I felt as if she was telling me more than what her words conveyed. I took a step towards her, held her tightly in my arms, brought myself close to her face, and kissed her on the lips. She was taken aback, seemed confused, and had an expression of shock. Leaving her gasping for words, I ran for my life. The rain had never been so strong and the winds never as wild. It seemed that the forces of nature were complementing and competing at the same time with the erogenous forces that had taken over me. There was no stopping, I swam up the gushing stream on the stairway, slipped through the auditorium lobby, and sprinted until I reached my room, to drop on my bed, my face down partly because of a feeling of triumph and partly because of a strange feeling of shame. I could hear my heartbeat loud and clear.

I didn't talk about this incident with anyone. The next day, I was sure Miss Tanya would complain to the Headmaster, then I would be caned in the morning assembly, humiliated in public for my boyish impulse, asked to read an apology, and subsequently rusticated from this lovely school. The whole night passed thinking about the repercussions that lay ahead. Every time I tried to sleep the Headmaster's square face would come devilishly in my dreams, a well-oiled cane by his side. I cursed myself. I asked myself what would my parents think? I questioned why I was even born? That night passed in a blink. The sun shone brightly the next morning. The trees looked freshly bathed in the rain. I left my bed with a heavy heart to face the consequences, knowing very well that even the Gods wouldn't save a boy who was in heat. The Gods only help kill the demons, and saving imprudent children in distress is not their priority or job. The school that day seemed to be a big cage in which a tender bird was jailed as a prisoner. In the lively environment where all the other birds were chirping in the happiness of going home, I was the only one who was burdened by my own misdeed.

At breakfast time, the school captain announced that the assembly had been canceled. I sighed with relief knowing the danger, the one of getting caned and humiliated in public, was over. Now, I did not want to be summoned at all. I immediately got into action, finished all discharge formalities, and rushed to the taxi waiting in the football ground near the tennis courts. Before I realised what was happening around me, I was at the railway station, on the train, and was soon sitting at home with my parents.

Sadly, at home too the nightmares of the headmaster running after me with a swishing cane in hand did not stop. One night, I dreamt of being expelled from the school and a letter was dispatched to inform my parents. From the very next day when everyone used to enjoy their afternoon siesta, I would sit on the gate waiting for the postman to arrive. And the postman did arrive soon with a letter from the school. I opened the envelope and unfolded the crisp page. It was not my expulsion letter but was my examination result. I presented the result to my father, who was happy about my grades, especially proud of the marks I got in Physics. I was also surprised, I had scored more than ninety-five percent marks. Miss Tanya's remarks on the sheet, "Well Done, Keep it Up!", meant more to me than it would to others.

Later, when the situation in the hills normalized, we returned to join the school. We learned on the first day that Miss Tanya had cleared the Civil Services Exam, and had left the school to pursue a glorious career.

I was happy. And, I was also sad. I still am.

TRAVELING TO OAK GROVE

~ Shrikant Avi

Now I come to the hills of Mussoorie as a tourist. Years ago, it was home.

In those days when we - my brother and I - were students of Oak Grove School, we used to travel by train. There used to be a lot of luggage: a trunk, a bedding, a tuck box, and a few extra handbags. Since we were two of us, it meant twice the luggage, and quadruple the agony of negotiation with other passengers in the train to fit our luggage under their seats. That was not all there was - we also used to fill the available passage near the compartment's toilets with our luggage!

Fortunately, most of the train used to be occupied by other

students of Oak Grove and their parents. Consequently, there was a tacit understanding amongst everyone that common areas will be occupied. I recall that the journey for most other passengers, who were not in the Oak Grove cohort of students and parents, was a nightmare - their spaces and minds encroached by us for the duration of their journey when they were packed in the compartment with us.

Back then, the train journey from my hometown to Oak Grove would take almost two complete days. We would start in the morning at Muzaffarpur, Bihar on the Barauni-Lucknow Express - our train of choice. At Lucknow, the next morning, we would have to change trains to Doon Express, since there was no direct train connecting Muzzaffarpur and Dehradun then.

At Muzaffarpur station, we would see a lot of Oak Grove people, our friends, and their families, since students from Bihar were represented formed a sizeable number of Oakgrovians. Once we were on board the train, we would incessantly urge our parents for permission to see our friends in the other compartments. The entire compartment used to be a fun-fair vibrant with social activities - family dinners, group meals, ludo, snake &

ladder, chess, cards, reading books, conversations, parents comparing notes on their ward's performance, and so on. The magnetic chessboard was a prized possession in those days. The valuable pieces on the chessboard were ardently protected from getting misplaced during jerks and jolts during the journey.

On reaching Lucknow, the second half of our expedition would commence. We were excited to see our other friends coming in from other cities and towns, adding to the numbers already from the Barauni-Lucknow Express. Our next ride would be the Doon Express train, which departed in the evening on the day. The waiting period would be spent by us ticking off a set list of activities in Lucknow - eating *kulfi* at Aminabad, shopping for *chikan* (traditional Lucknow embroidery) clothes, and savouring lunch at a preferred restaurant. Each time there would be a debate on whether to take away the dinner from the restaurant. The alternative was to order from the pantry on the train. I always sided with the pantry meal, which was my preferred Indian Thali. While we discussed and debated, we would be mindful of the time required to move our voluminous luggage from the station that we landed from Barauni to the station from which Doon Express would depart. Lucknow had two train stations next to each other.

Doon Express reached Dehradun in the morning, the day after. A few families, who were typically always in a hurry, made their wards wear the school uniform in the train itself. My family was unusually relaxed in such matters. My parents slept on their berths till the train had halted at Dehradun and the jostling coolies hurried in to pick the luggage. The coolies would lug our bags and holdalls to the nearby Railway Rest House. There we freshened up and got ready for the rest of the day ahead of us. The cold water of Dehradun prompted a reminder from my parents to be adequately covered at all times with woollens during the stay in school.

My family had their priority clearly defined, and it was to not get to the school immediately, but to shop. Basmati rice, bakery products and woollen clothes were the essentials that we picked up from select shops in Dehradun. When the shopping was done, we had our lunch at one of the preferred restaurants near the railway station. My brother and I used to get anxious seeing our friends zoom past us one by one in the taxis. We would pester our parents and eventually force them to hurry.

I fretted about how painful the entire process of registration at the school would be. The first stop was the dormitory supervisor, then the housemaster, thereafter the hospital, and eventually the M.O.D. (Master on Duty). If we got there late, the entire process was much more troublesome, as the queues, lunch & tea breaks delayed the whole registration further. The registration at the Boys' school was faster, however, my brother's in Junior school would take twice as much time. In Junior school, one had to tally the toothpaste, cold cream, bottles of hair oil, Vaseline, clothes, tuck box essentials and much more things in front of the school staff and matron. So much had to be done, and here were my parents, relishing the food in the restaurant near the railway station!

Finally, when we traveled up from the Doon Valley towards our school. At a certain point during the journey, a chill in the breeze would make us realise that the vacations were over, and the next six months of the year would be with friends, teachers and staff, amidst the oak trees. The next six months were to be spent making wonderful memories, which I cherish to this day.

These days when we come to Mussoorie, we take the road

and have only one, at most two, backpacks for luggage. The spirit of a vacation may be ascertained by how the traveler feels, and backpacks always make you feel like a tourist. Therefore, these days, I come to the hills of Mussoorie as a tourist. Back then, it was like reaching home.

8 YEARS IN LOCKDOWN
~ *Priyanka Pandey*

For my siblings and me, an argument a day is very normal. I assume such is the case with all siblings. However, sometimes I feel we fight over the most frivolous matters. Only yesterday, I was having a heated discussion on whether or not we should send our children to a boarding school. I was advocating for it while my sister was against it. Our discussion went on until when her five month old child had to perpetuate a throaty intervention, and we ended our argument by disconnecting the phone. I call our discussion frivolous since I am yet to have children, and my sister's is barely a few months old.

The discussion took me, down the memory lane, to a place

where I loved to wander around huge stone walls, long corridors, and giant oak trees. I remember complaining in the third standard to one of my friends '*Yaar yeh bhi kaisi life hai, ghantiyon se bandhi hui? Bell baje toh utho, bell baje to khao, bell baje to padho aur bell baje so jao. (What kind of life is this, tied to the ringing of bells? Up when it rings, study when it does, and finally sleep when it rings again.)* 'Is this really the way of life we are going to follow for the next 8 years?'. Immediately thereafter the bell rang, and we laughed as there was not much we could do about it and we headed for the dining hall to have our evening snacks.

In my boarding school, we had a schedule for every minute of the day; even our personal time was scheduled. How I used to complain about it back then and, how deeply I miss it now. Those eight years of my life were the best ones and I look forward to any chance of revisiting those days.

I remember my first day at Oak Grove School, it was the 21st of April, 1995. The entire batch of the third standard had joined on the 20th April and I was a day late. After the eye test that caused the delay, I joined the school donning a fat pair of spectacles. Oh! It was fun, the floor looked bouncy from behind the glasses and I definitely felt like the doctor I wanted to be when I grew up.

That day, there was a hailstorm and the weather was too cold for the month of April. It felt like that then because I came from a town in Uttar Pradesh called Tundla where anything beyond *Holi[1]* meant summer. My parents, siblings, grandfather, uncle, aunt, who had all come down to see me off, and myself sat under a covered shed of the Junior School. All the joining formalities were completed, and they were going to hand me over to my class teacher. I do not recall feeling scared, but I can remember that my parents didn't seem overjoyed as I thought they would be. I was the naughtiest one amongst my siblings and assumed that getting rid of me would make their life easier but I learned that such is usually not the case with parents. They were going to miss me, and this realisation gave me a strange feeling. I felt the tears welling up in my eyes. I did not want to cry, not in front of everyone, not just yet.

Papa held me close and said, '*achche se rehna aur padhai karna, teachers ko takleef mat dena. Mein har week letter likhunga*' (*Stay well, study and don't trouble your teachers. I will write to you every week*). He then led me to my class. I felt the tears welling up in my eyes. I did not want to cry,

---

1. *Holi - the festival of colours marking the beginning of spring in India*

not in front of everyone, not yet.

The first day went by rapidly. There were so many new faces to register, I got tired of it and went back to thinking about my siblings, who were excited about their tour to Haridwar after dropping me to school. 'So selfish of them to go visiting places without me,' I said to myself feeling a bit jealous. Could I cry now? No, no, not yet, I did not want to be one who cried.

By the end of the first week I was all set with the new routine. A bell would ring at 5:30 am to wake us up, when we would freshen up. *Ammajis* would assist the 3rd standard girls - standards 4th and 5th were old enough to do it themselves. We would line up for our bath and by 6:30 am, we would be ready in our sports uniform to go down to the field for physical training (basic exercises). The bell at 7:30 am would signal the end of the session, and we had half an hour to freshen up again and change into our school uniforms. 8 am was the bell for breakfast, when we would line up and move to the dining room. Till date, the aroma of porridge brings back memories of the school to this day. A bell at 8:30 a.m., meant morning assembly, after which were the bells for different subject classes, then lunch, followed once again for classes. Evening snacks were at 4 p.m., after which we were done with the school hours, but not with the bells.

A bell for playtime, followed by a bell for self study, a bell for dinner, a bell for self study again, a bell to freshen up at the dormitory and finally a bell to sleep. On weekends, when we did not have classes, the bells still signalled us for afternoon play and sleep.

I had not cried yet, but sudden bursts of this emotion would bubble up regularly. I had to constantly suppress it. I was settling in so well, making new friends and I could not be stupid enough to stutter and spoil it all.

One day after breakfast, a newly made friend came to me and said, 'Hey Pandey, where is your other earring? Have you lost it?'

'What?' I touched my ears, and one ring was indeed missing. I never removed it, where could it go? Did it fall while I was having a bath? What would I do? Mummy had told me to take good care of my things. The hole in my ear might close. Oh no! What now? What do I do? Who do I tell? I could speak about something like this to mummy, but she wasn't here. WHO DO I TELL? I could not control it any further.

It took them 11 days but my tears finally burst out in a flood, and I cried bitterly. A few seniors came to my rescue, they tried asking me what went wrong. My friend explained, 'she has lost her earring *didi*'. I could hear everyone consoling me, telling me that they would look for it, that I was a strong girl and shouldn't cry. Well, maybe I was strong but not strong enough. Not yet.

After these initial hiccups, my life at school started getting better, and more fun actually. Weeks turned into months and then years. We would go back home for vacations every five months. Parents could visit and take us out on weekends too. Since my home town was not really close by - more than an overnight journey - my parents would make it once in two months, to take me out for a day or two and that felt good. I always looked forward to it. We started learning to deal with our emotions, to confide in friends, solve our own problems and most importantly adapt to any situation.

I moved to Senior School in the 6th standard. It had its own set of challenges and fun. Our relationship with the school bell continued. How quick 8 years flew by? Before we realised, it was time for the final goodbye. It felt like I was leaving behind a part of my life. All I had ever known was to live in my school, with my schoolmates and my teachers; now I wondered how life outside those stone walls would be. Would I be able to settle down in the world outside these walls?

On the day, leaving formalities were completed. I was waiting with Papa at Dehradun Railway Station for our train, which would take us home and into the world I felt I had never known. I felt the tears welling up in my eyes. I did not want to cry, not in front of everyone, not yet.

BIG MA'AM

~ Nikhil Kumar

It was after twenty years, in the year Big Ma'am passed away, that I started eating eggs again. My relationship with eggs had ended soon after I joined Oak Grove (OG) in 1995. On the first day at OG many of the new students were ushered inside Class 3B, which, as I found later, would be the section I would study in. In comparison to other classes, 3B was the biggest. On Sundays, the empty portion of the classroom — behind the orderly desks — doubled up as the TV room. It had big, clear glass windows looking out to a flat, corralled by crenelated *pushta*, where sometimes girls went to play. At daytime, despite the grove of oaks beyond the pushta, the windows allowed the dappled sunlight through the dark green leaves and grey trunks; but on April 20th in 1995, at

6 p.m., it was dark. A sheet of rain, earlier in the day, had chagrined the reluctant sun to be enfolded in a transient embrace.

The new students were made to sit in the tube-lit class; two to each desk. I was not used to tube-lights. In the railway quarters at Gaya, where I came from, we only used bulbs; or lanterns when power went: an event that occurred often. Earlier in the evening, my parents and siblings had left me with Miss Thapa, one of the two matrons for boys in Junior School (JS). Near my bed, where I was handed over, I cried and hugged one by one my parents, brother, and little sister. My nine-year old eyes were still moist when I sat in the old oak double desk under the unyielding white light surrounded by an unknown group of children. Some of them knew the place, as I could gather from their conversation. They, later, clarified that they were from Class 5.

One of them was Gunjan Masoom. A fair, short guy with a high angular forehead. When I think of him now, the image of Edward G Robinson comes to mind, not his villainy though. He was kind to us with very little air about him, despite the novel seniority ordained on him and his classmates as the senior-most class in Junior School.

Masoom was holding forth on what lay ahead for us. His best friend, Mritunjay — he with *laddoos* instead of cheeks — was talking to my other classmates.

It was Masoom who told us, on that first Jharipani evening, about Big Ma'am and Ma'am. Adding 'small' would have made it euphonious, but less respectful, one suspects. Although Mrs. Bhaskar and Mrs. Khanna – Big Ma'am and Ma'am –, if one looked at them, could have easily been categorised as big and small; also, in terms of the terror they triggered. The other teachers were merely Misses. Later, we heard the suave Boys School (BS) seniors referring to the Misses as Ma'ams. That was their word, not meant for us lowly, regimented JS chicks. My uncle, who I looked up to as my style guru, had taught me to use Ma'am for women teachers. It was more stylish, he had said. But now I was not in Gaya. It was Mussoorie hills. Things would go, as they do, in the good tradition of a hundred-year-old institution.

***

I have never kept a journal. Some classmates kept diaries in Junior School. I do not know what became of them. In absence of records, what can one remember of a person, but scenes and fragments. Memory is a disloyal device and time its accomplice. Come to think of it, the story of our lives could even be the stories we have forgotten.

I can remember few other things that happened in 1995, but no memory of that year carries the epochal sense than that of being caned in the corridor. It must have been July, or August, because I remember wearing Duckback Gumboots. This utilitarian footwear I had only encountered in the form of Galoshes in Enid Blyton books, but had never seen or worn them and was harried to find it listed among fourteen shirts and six slacks in the OG prospectus brought by my father. To make matters worse it was not even available in the best shoe shops of Gaya. The kit consisting of clothes, shoes, toiletries etc. had to be brought from home and they were thoroughly inspected by the matrons after every vacation. Of course, there were several unnecessary items, and I felt the gumboots were the most unnecessary. I was given the half Wellington variety and every monsoon it would tear near the big toe. For the three years I was in JS, my father kept buying a new pair at Dehra with his meagre Railway salary.

Prep happened between 6 to 7 p.m.. That day Priyanka, a

prefect, was sent to monitor my class. She was a looker; the prettiest among all the Class 5 girls. As a prefect you had an authority, but it was not always summoned to great extents. The boys, at that time though, felt the girl prefects favoured their gender by allowing them more freedom, or overlooking their acts of indiscipline.

A few minutes after the prep started, I went up to Priyanka, who was sitting on the teachers' chair, to seek permission to go to the toilet. She refused. It was perhaps not improper on her part, as she did not know my condition and boys could hardly be trusted. I came back to my seat and tried to put myself to reading. The waters in the bladder continued to rumble. Priyanka ambled, book in hand, between the rows of desks. Distracted by the internal situation and her sauntering, my eyes veered towards the window. Yet, it did not help forget, and forgetting helps, as I learned later. The art of controlling to wee-wee was still a few years' practice away. I stood up, as she came near my desk, to ask; only to be refused again. Now, the penny needed to be spent urgently. After wriggling for a few minutes, I devised a plan. This time, I sought permission to sharpen my pencil. She allowed that. The idea was to make a surreptitious escape while sharpening the pencil, which was done near the bin placed behind the door that exited in the corridor. But alas, as things happen, my plan did not come to fruition. The clouds bursting at the seams could not survive a few seconds of movement. Frozen at the bin, with a sharpener and pencil in hand, I felt a warm stream run down my hairless thighs, half of it entering the half Wellington and the rest trickling down the trousers towards the bin, making a surreptitious escape outside. I stood there like a rock dreading when Priyanka would ask me to go back. Standing there for so long would, no doubt, make her smell a rat, but how do you turn about in piddled pants?

Ms. Bhatia, who was the class teacher for 3B, was the MoD (Master/Mistress on Duty) that day. Seeing the puddle in the corridor, she came inside the class. I was still behind the door, feeling comforted by the bin. One glance at me and she understood what had happened. Taking me by the ear, out in the corridor – pencil still in hand – led me straight to the dormitory to change. She, in a sense, had saved me.

From the corner of my eye I saw the amorphous beauty I had created. It was like a detritus island of water on concrete, or a giant spatula, the front of which had melted with overheating. "All forms of beauty", as Baudelaire has written, "like all possible phenomena, have within them something eternal and something transitory — an absolute and a particular element." Mine was an abstraction too, combined with an absolute and transitory. Often, afterwards, when I have crossed that area of the corridor, I have tried to imagine the little boy standing at the door and the contours of his long-evaporated piss.

When I returned from the dorm, the school had queued up for dinner. My class had given respectful space to my creation. As the queue started to move for the dining hall, the boys passed by, but did not cross by hopping over, as if, doing that would stunt its future scope. I stood behind Shitikantha, the last person in the queue, although being the second shortest boy of Class 3, I would usually stand second. Like the rest of the class, I tread the same path as those who went before – making a right turn and then a left, observing that melted spatula for one last time.

I, like a bride, had my dinner with eyes cast down; trying hard to not think of what was in the offing.

Big Ma'am came to the dining hall, as she did every night. I was aware even with downcast eyes. She must have seen it before it was wiped off and she must have asked the MoD about it.

The next day was Sunday. After breakfast, on Sundays, we were moved in the class for an hour-long prep, post which we went out on the flat to play. Monsoons are the season of *futta* or football in Jhids (short for Jharipani in senior Boys School argot), a sport I have never been fond of. On the days, our class got to play *futta*, I would sit in the Covered Shed and watch seniors play table-tennis (TT). Class 3 kids seldom got a chance to play TT but observation is a great teacher, and it helped me pick up the game later on. The two ping-pong tables were placed at one end of the Covered Shed. Along the stout pillars were cast iron benches on which the day's newspapers were kept. I read them with gusto, but with sparing comprehension, as I had at Gaya – reading the newspaper to my grandfather before or after his work hours.

Monthly tests were not far, but I used the prep to think of West Indies touring England: of Lara's drives and Ambrose's wickets. My reverie was broken when Big Ma'am entered the class with grey, long, open hair, a cane and a fresh breeze that turned into pain and is now lodged in my mind as memory.

She called and took me out in the corridor. I received two whacks on the calves. The cane, perhaps made of rattan — and I would not be surprised if it had been passed from headmistress to headmistress — was quite elastic and Big Ma'am applied an adequate amount of thrust for it to cause an adequate amount of pain. I was not scolded; she did not say anything. It was like a bloodless coup. We understood what was done and what must not be done again.

That was my first major encounter with Big Ma'am. It would not be long before I would be caned again. And this time for doing something I had not actually done.

***

Breakfast in JS was at 8, and 8:30 on Sundays. The non-vegetarians got porridge, two slices of bread, butter, tea, and an egg. The egg would either be hard-boiled, scrambled or beaten into an omelette. At home, I used to have eggs, but with not as much relish as my elder brother did. He could pour down the white and the yolk with minimum effort in his mouth or ravish the wobbly poach at a corner *thela*. He was discernibly delighted when I told him during the summer vacation that I ate an egg every day, and ex cathedra told me to continue doing so.

I cannot now put a finger on when I became allergic to eggs. It was perhaps a Friday of October; Friday because the dinner roster had egg curry. Waking up late at night in a paroxysm, I vomited beside my bed. The stomach-ache had begun soon after dinner in the dorm and had felt like someone had put a clip on my intestines and passed current in it. Choosing to stay shut, I slept off after brushing my teeth and polishing my shoes, thinking sleep would heal, as it often did. My bed was near the door that led to the night guard's room. Seen from the main entry of the dorm, it was at the other end, a little short of the corner on the right. The night guard's room, I learnt afterwards, used to be Ma'am Khanna's room before she married. It was the room where a love was born.

I did not tell anyone in the morning either. The pain had vanished instantly after I had slovenly chundered the whole enchilada. Under the soft haze of the cobalt night bulb, I washed off the vomit from the floor, bringing water from the toilet and splashing it out of the door towards the night guard's room. But I missed the stains on my bedsheet.

In the morning, I made my bed, dressed up and went downstairs. The day passed peacefully. When night fell, Miss Thapa enquired what I had done. Despite my honest admission, she had made up her mind that it was not vomit, but shit. The presence of water had perhaps circumstantiated her convictions; and perhaps my history. As I returned to my bed after a slap from Miss Thapa, I thought it would only be a matter of time before Big Ma'am, if she didn't already, would come to know. The inner chamber of my dread made me lose sleep that night, even though my bed had been spread with a fresh white sheet.

Next day was Sunday, but nothing happened. I did not know then that Monday would prove to be bloody.

In the morning assembly, after the songs and prayers, Big Ma'am called out my name. From behind the ping pong tables, Bachchan Singh with a big black moustache and dark eyes, came with the cane. My maroon full sleeved jersey hung loose, as fashion dictated, hiding my buttocks. Big Ma'am said something about the importance of discipline to the assembly as she delicately folded up my jersey. With all the teachers, girls, and boys watching, I received three. Smarting, I grit my teeth, but flinched as little as I could muster, for I was not wrong.

The temporary stain of the bedsheet had led to temporary marks on my butt and indelible ones in the folds of my mind. As further punishment, my playtime for a week was suspended; I was to sit outside Big Ma'am's office. Most people did not know why I was caned; that day in the assembly, there were a few more—a couple of Class 5 boys and a girl—who were served the same dessert. The girl's caning was conspicuously overwhelming as the boys forgot to ask me what I had done. Those who did, received a cold stare as an answer. Only close friends knew the truth.

I was not anguished by Big Ma'am's caning though. Earlier, I was the guy who had pissed his pants, but now I was not the one who had shat. The second caning was like the second coming. To be caned twice in Class 3 was as badass as it could get. If in no one else's, at least in my own mind, I had arrived.

***

Octobers in Mussoorie are sensuous. The hills, bounded in by the Winterline, seem more intimate. The fulgent patterns of sunlight make the days all glare and verdant. In the evenings, a crimson sky cuts you deep, whirling within you, a parliament of voices: wanted or unwanted.

The cast-iron bench with sacramento green slats, on which I was supposed to sit for a week, was outside Big Ma'am's office. From that coign of vantage, in the gloaming of an October evening, I looked out to a dainty, dignified and rarely seen area of the school; an area that was the most well-kept in all of Oak Grove. In Junior School, we could only enter it during Founders' Day with buntings to welcome the chief guest. The colourful buntings had to be held in both hands and waved above the head. As if that were not hard enough, the May sun of Mussoorie — subdued in comparison to plains — with its unadulterated transmission, was punishing. Performing the bunting-charade for an uninspiring *sarkari babu* every year seemed especially pointless. At such a time, the beauty of the place was lost on me, sitting in the glow of my thoughts for a week, the bewitching charm of that place had me in its thrall.

The bench was under the coarse stone edifice that had iron columns, wooden trusses, a red tin roof — congruent to the British period, but with a character of its own. Richard

Roskell Bayne, the architect of the first building of Oak Grove, was dead by the time Junior School began to be built, but he had laid the foundation of the design that Railway engineers followed. JS was set in a flat or perhaps a flattened patch of hill in which grew pine and oak. Amidst these trees on one side was a turf tennis court and a lawn. The lawn was full of bright flowers: geraniums, zinnias, coneflowers, goat's beard, sedges and ferns and some others whose name I regret to have not learnt. A gardener could be seen with a sprinkling can in hand moving among the flower beds belted by bricks. *Bajri* was used in patches that looked uncannily pretty.

The air smelled faintly of pines, and a sense of pining wafted. It was here that Big Ma'am lived, on the floor above her office. It was also from here, I later learnt, that a young BS teacher, jumped from the first floor onto the flat, not finding any other escape, during a whirlwind affair with a JS teacher. As school children we are curious for the forbidden. We seldom want to know how one lives, or what loneliness is. Not because we do not want to, but perhaps because we are yet to become cognizant of such realities. I did not know then, and I do not know now, what Big Ma'am's life was like outside of her work. What movies she saw; what music she heard; what books she read; or who she talked to. I, at least, never saw her conversing with other teachers, which could be construed as a friendly chat. She laughed, but hardly in front of us. There is a photograph of her with Boys School students taken on *Holi*. Clad in a white *salwar kameez*, a light vermilion *dupatta*, she has a small *gulal tika* on her forehead. The head tilts slightly to the right and a languorous smile escapes her lips. The boys and Big Ma'am stand in the girls' flat of JS. She has both her hands in front; the left clasping the right. An article on body language in a magazine said that such a posture can be taken to mean the person is vulnerable but is required to display confidence.

Like many things, even her full name was unbeknownst to me until much later. Her signature is imprinted in my mind. The words formed fully and beautifully in her cursive hand, clearly pronounced the S, the B, and the Bhaskar of her name, which meant Shubh Bala Bhaskar. We saw the signature in our report cards, or in the dictation sheet. Big Ma'am did not teach any particular subject, but she would take the dictation test for half yearly and final exam. The dictation was something of an event. She read a passage, enunciated with perfect pauses, that we had to grasp and write down; then, she would give five words. One wrong spelling cost three marks of the total fifty. I remember scoring forty-four most of the time and a fifty once. Some classmates could not figure out what she said and muffed up the spellings; the blame for which should fall on their nerves more than their comprehension.

During the prayer ceremony held after her passing in June 2015, I got a glimpse of her inner life. Rakesh Sharma, her son in law, spoke of the first time he visited Jharipani before his marriage in the early 80s. It was a misty August evening. Her room was clean, things perfectly placed, and when he got up after tea and introductions, the trace of his presence was eliminated before he could realise. Mr. Sharma was then taken for a round of the school, which also had everything at the right place. Dressing gowns — hundreds of them — exactly in the same order. Toothbrushes dangling in a strange symmetry. Basins clean, even at their bases. His epigrammatic remark that Mrs. Bhaskar must have given grief to those who worked under her or those she taught lightened up the austere occasion. After her retirement, she spent a life devoted to her parents, her brother, and her family. Her younger brother was a prominent business personality — Y C Deveshwar of ITC Ltd. —, about whom, again we did not know until much after school. Mr. Sharma let us know that she filed every picture and article on her brother that appeared in the media.

Authority figures need distance and she was an apt exemplar. All of us — the students, the teachers, the staff — who crossed her path, evinced awe or fear, or both. Love came afterwards. As little boys, who did not think themselves to be little, feared her; her sheer energy, her immensity, her grey-silvery hair neatly tied, her stylishly muted saree perfectly pleated, her voice clanging from end to end of the corridor, and those piercing eyes. Her orderliness and the fear she elicited, educed a sort of irritation. Many of us, including the staff, awaited her superannuation. Looking back and looking at Oak Grove that it is now, I wish Big Ma'am had never retired. Better still, I wish she were a never-aging phantom or one that spawned a never-ending line of Big Ma'ams to serve the little hamlet of Jharipani.

A small incident that speaks for my dislike of Big Ma'am, at that time, occurred when I returned after the winter vacations of Class 4 in February of 1997. There was a long queue, in front of her office, to complete the formalities of our reporting back to school. The queue chugged along as did the parents standing beside their wards. Someone in the front bent down to touch her feet. Everyone followed to do the same thenceforth. That winter, my uncle had come to drop me, as my father had taken ill, and my grandfather although he wanted to come, could not. When my turn came, I did not bend down to touch her feet. There were two reasons: one, this was not in the tradition of Oak Grove — I explained to myself later; second, I did not want to, because I did not like her. My uncle did not approve of my behaviour, as it seemed from his question, but the moment of his departure was near and he left me with the advice that generosity and love last, dislike doesn't.

***

After two days of sitting alone on the bench, I was joined by a Class 5 senior. He was the tallest guy, but neither great at sports nor studies. S C Gupta, or SC to us, would bloom as an artist and as a long-distance runner in BS. SC believed Big Ma'am couldn't stand him, and therefore, although he was not the only one talking, he had been singled out. I chuckled and said that I had been punished for shitting, and he for bullshitting. SC remained loquacious. The last time I met him was at Ganga Dhaba in JNU. His long screed was about why one should never fall in love especially with

Delhi girls. Soon after that he got married, which I heard was not an arranged one. SC made for an interesting company on the bench. He knew a lot of things about things and he liked to talk about them. We became friends and he helped me in BS as much as he could.

After the vomiting incident, my bed was shifted. It was now in the Class 5 row, just one away from the window. My neighbour was Sanjeev Singh, a new joiner in Class 5, who would later go on to become a national record holder in 100 metre dash, and the school captain. Sanjeev and I would talk a lot after the lights were switched off. He was the one, who, when I was admitted in the hospital in Class 4th, taught me the word 'fuck'.

Every night, I would leave the curtains of Sanjeev's window slightly ajar; enough for me to see the night sky and difficult enough for Miss Thapa to notice. I loved looking at the spectral moon, and the two sets of stars – one hung low in the sky and the other haphazardly arranged on the Mussoorie hills. Some nights the tired moon cast its pale light through the mullion and transom, making a nice frame; and on others it did not appear perhaps shrouded by the oaks. On those nights, the illuminated hill would keep me in trance till sleep came embracing. There were moonless nights too, and crickets, who stridulated their everlasting monotonous meaningful note. Droplets of water played the musical solfège. Sometimes, the breeze softened by the mighty oaks would enter the dorm, soothing my loneliness away. And in those hours, out of the front door Big Ma'am would enter with her elves. Inside the quilt tightly tucked in the mattress I played dead, eyes shut, but ears wide open trying to hear the soft murmur in the pitter-patter of walking shoes.

I often think of those nights and try to conjure up those footsteps. It makes me wonder if we can ever leave the places, we have grown up in.

It was only in the last hour of the morning of 30th June 2015 that I read of the passing of Big Ma'am. She had closed her eyes at 5:52 a.m. in the presence of her family.

I had last seen her in March 1998. She had retired on the last day of February—her birthday month but stayed back for a few more days. It was also the penultimate month for my class in JS before we went to the senior schools; a quaint period, if there ever was one. A winter of hope and happiness was passing, as a spring of despair and fear awaited us. We would be delivered from Junior School to the Senior Boys (and Senior Girls). To go from the abandon of a Class 5 senior to the horror of a Class 6 chick is a *rite de passage* more defined than any other in the life of an Oakgrovian.

I do not know how, but Big Ma'am had prepared us. She was like the mountain, who by its sheer presence teaches you.

Now, when I think of her, I am reminded of a poem:

Even after all this time
the sun never says to the earth,
"You owe me."
Look what happens with
a love like that,
it lights the whole sky.

She lit up our lives with her being.

This tribute was written in October 2017.

SINGING SIBLINGS
~ *Kanishka Mallick*

Since a very young age we had people around at home who appreciated music. Mother was a good, but shy singer; typical of the women of that era. She would have these infrequent *Rabindra Sangeet* hiccups: explaining what Mr. Tagore meant in the same musical flow before going silent again, suddenly. Father was a surprise. His singing talent came to be known to us, rather late in life. I guess, he too was a reticent performer. I suspect we found out about his talent much later, as he would emulate Elvis on one extreme and Talat Mehmood on the other. At the tender age that we were, we did not know if he was trying to scare the crows off our verandah! My introduction into the world of rhythm, rhyme, lyrics and melody was through my sister.

Before we could make sense of the world, we were shipped to a boarding school. To be fair, I am told, I had violently volunteered to be sent out. My sister had been sent to boarding school in Mussoorie in 1986. The family had traveled to drop her. I had instantly fallen in love with the place. The train journey, early morning sighting of mountains at a far distance from the train right up until the point we were driving up one. Lush green hills, suddenly vanishing in the hide and seek of clouds and fog. It took us a while to differentiate between the two. Chilly mornings, warm afternoons, pleasant summer evenings and cosy cold nights. It was heaven. My sister, who had joined the school a year before was a really popular singer by the time I joined. Our music teacher took a chance on me only because we shared the same family name. I was discovered only because of my elder sister. To confess, I dedicate my singing star status only to her.

But before that, another embedded parallel storyline. In 1987, as a new joiner, I was loitering around visibly not so happy with something that I cannot seem to remember now. Someone called me and gave me a chance to hit a few shuttles with the Badminton racquet. I did. So hard that the racquet gutting gave away. This was in what we called the flat, a pebble-surfaced (*bajree*) area, used as a playing field. Now that we were one racquet short, some of the young ones whispered something and went about in different directions. Only later was I made party to their begging plan. One boy would go and beg for a racquet from the girls' flat at the far end. One boy would go and beg for a racquet from the other section of the same class. The most influential boy would be sent to beg, borrow or blackmail a racquet from the Games Captain. Mostly, no one succeeded. The Ma'am on Duty (*MOD*) would usually intervene with a promise of a new one in the coming days. Anyhow, boys went about looking for a replacement racquet. Being the fresh one, I was not tasked with anything, except being warned and made responsible to never part with the shuttle in our possession. Else, the next begging plan would need bigger, bolder moves and may involve the usual beg, borrow or steal! I had limited understanding of the geographic importance of hot spots around the campus. So, I strayed straight into the indoor badminton court (*service hall*) where students from Senior School (*senior boys and senior girls separately on different days and dates*) used to come to play Badminton. I was unaware of these facts until I saw the marked-out badminton court on the floor inside the hall. But instead of players what I saw was a group of children sitting around a few musical instruments. Naturally, I was intrigued and doubled up to get closer to them. Suddenly, I felt a jolt on my shoulder. Mrs. Sushila Tyagi/Pandey *(musical accompaniments and dance teacher)* held me tight by the shoulder and announced, "Look who is here! Jayanti's brother!"

As if that was not embarrassing enough, Mrs. Anuradha Sharma *(music teacher)* announced without any warning, "Come here, sit with me and sing something for us!" I felt like the roof blasting open and a bright white light sucking me into the skies. There was complete silence in the hall with the kids looking at me in anticipation and the music teachers with their encouraging smiles and nods. The wait seemed endless. I did manage to mumble a few words. Once I ended my lines, what felt like cold breathless moments after a sharp object buckles you down, there was pin drop silence. A loud roar of applause followed. At that age, my good guess is, I may have peed a little in my grey terrycot trousers in those frightened moments. Disbelievingly, Mrs. Sharma offered me to sing the lead song in the forthcoming *Janmashtami* celebrations. From the very next day onwards, I distanced myself from the begging boys gang and would walk straight into the Badminton courts, for music rehearsals. When my sister got to know, she was ecstatic. Naturally, she was not declaring that her brother was singing during *Janmashtami*. She was yelling, "*my brother can sing!!*"

There would be roughly a dozen kids during rehearsals. I knew the whole junior school would be attending the function on the same badminton courts. On D-day, the 200 pairs of eyes, staring blankly, made me sick in the stomach. My throat dried down, toes went numb and I could start hearing whispers and soft giggles against my already vibrating eardrums. I tried to find my sister in the crowd for some solace, totally forgetting she was in the same singing group sitting fairly close to me. I was too scared and equally embarrassed to look at her either. However, once Mrs. Tyagi's harmonium gave the starting key, being a *bhajan*, I closed my eyes and pretended I was feeling devotional. I was praying, no doubt. The reasons were very different! To confess, I may have half-peed that day too!

My first public song, which gave me instant stardom was, "*Papa kehte hain, bada naam karega*". I am sure, like all fathers, my father used to believe the same too. He gave up soon. It was my sister, her various talents and personality that gave me future opportunities and the ability to take risks later. It was from her that I got the confidence to sing in and for a crowd. My sister is a supreme performer. Yes, she has been the conventional "*Big Bully*" sister. I simply adore her. I have come across very few people with her kind of single-minded focus, dedication and diligence to achieve something one aspires for. And of course, I love her singing. Ok, to confess finally, I love her.

THE SECRET NO MORE

~ Amit Suri

Not all incidents in life can be bared outright. There are sacred secrets in a few, which if revealed before it's time, may cause unwarranted flurry. I harbour one such secret that I wish to share now, just over thirty years later after the incident. I am now ready to face the consequences of my defection.

Those of you who have been in boarding schools surely know well of the secrets that remain shielded between the seniors and the juniors, the staff and the students, the boys and the girls, during the light of the day and hidden in the dark of the night. It makes no sense to open Pandora's box but someone must rise above, muster the courage and reveal the truth - a truth that is shrouded perhaps in an untold story, narrated decades later than never ever.

The boarding school I studied at in my childhood spread over acres of land covering a few green mountains, several undulating slopes, many aesthetic structures, a majestic valley, and an angelic waterfall too. To this day, it is home to an abundance of Oak trees and supports myriad species of flora and fauna in its lushness and life-nourishing shades. This secret, which I am going to reveal to you today, hatched on a Sports Day in the late 1980s. That day the whole of the boarding school had busied itself preparing for the big event. There were three of us who are witnesses to what transpired on that day away from the eyes of the others. We three kept mum, not out of fear, but because the boarding school boys never rat out their comrades. I choose to defect now - call me a 'sneaker' if you must, but a man's gotta do what a man's gotta do, before it's too late!

We, the children of boarding schools all across the world, know in our heart that there is a clear demarcation among us when we define the sporting-index of each of us. There are those who are good at a particular sport, and those who are not good at any. Among the ones who 'are not', there is a further implicit classification - the ones who are 'short and rounded', and therefore not good for any physical activity; and the ones who are 'big and burly', with unfavourable Body Mass Index 'BMI', thus making them incompetent for the right Sports-category they could participate in, yet they are good to carry out menial laborious tasks.

Though seldom expressed explicitly, the children of boarding school also tacitly understand that for the proper functioning of the hostel routine, all livestock with jelly between their ears, whether 'short and rounded' or 'big and burly', must be put to its optimal use. Therefore, the livestock that is good at a Sport prepares for the relevant track or field event, while the remaining ones are engaged in the preparation of banners, pom-poms, cheer-leading thingies, glorified speeches, etc. The worst livestock, the one in which yours truly belongs to this day, the class which shelters 'big and burly', the ones with the undesirable 'BMI', is good to prepare the fields with the markings of *'chuna'* (powdered limestone), and coolie the goods from the warehouses across the campus to the central valley where the Sports events unfold. The warehouses were typically located in the remotest corners tucked in the three hundred acres of the school compound. If required, which I may add is *always* required, this group is also expected to trim the blades of grass to the right size lest the Sporty livestock may slip, stumble, or stagnate at their hour of glory.

Having built the premise, I believe it is now time that I must spill the beans and reveal the well-guarded secret without testing your patient eyes and ears any more. I remember vividly that on that Sports Day, Zahir, Pippy, and I were assigned to ferry the sacks laden with '*chuna*' from the warehouse near the front-pitch at the top of the mountain to '*our glorious valley green*' down below. Though the three of us may have been the right people for the job, though with the wrong BMI for that day, this task of ferrying the sacks was by all standards humanly, a bally mean one. The limestone sacks were heavy, made more so with the morning dew and drizzle adding kilos to it. While we contemplated on tactical details of how to do the job with the least effort, we knew in our heart that time was of the essence to escape the wrath of the Sports Captain - a burly, bitter and brusque baddy, known for targetted barking on kinder souls for getting any job done.

At that moment, the wise Pippy - the one who was a repository of bright ideas and also with the unblemished distinction of continuous streak of 'first in the class' grades - noticed an inviting wheelbarrow parked nearby. It takes little imagination to know what one could do next. We put a few sacks of limestone onto the barrow and gleefully rolled from the top of the mountain to the valley down below.

On our way down, it was Zahir's idea that one of us could even sit on the barrow and take a ride! Pippy immediately grabbed the offer and hopped onto the barrow while Zahir and I steered the vehicle skillfully from near the Principal's office to the destination point, a path with a steep slope which made the barrow-ride adventurous for its occupant. What fun it was! The view of the Doon valley on the left side, the cool whiff of air in our hair, and the pleasant chill of the onsetting winters made the ride spectacular as the barrow rattled down the sylvan sloping path guided ably by two 'big and burly' chappies with the undesirable BMI.

We emptied the sacks in the valley and gleefully pushed the light wheelbarrow up for the next consignment. At the warehouse on top of the hill, the vehicle was stocked again with the cargo. This time Zahir was the new passenger while Pippy and I captained the ride to the destination. A job which would have taken half an hour, or more, was now being done in less than a fourth of its time, and that too with ease and pleasure. We, the three of us, were as happy as a clam at the high tide!

The next ride had me in the passenger's seat while Pippy and Zahir controlled the barrow. I remember to this day how I was loving it - cool air in my head, and the scenic view of Doon valley on my left. The vehicle gained momentum and my heartbeat picked pace in tandem. The barrow was gliding down fast and I was beginning to get scared with rumbling sounds forming in my belly. I shouted to slow down but the barrow kept getting faster and faster. I held tight the front rim of the barrow and turned around my neck to bark orders to Pippy and Zahir to slow down, but to my shock, both the able-bodied men were missing at the helm!

It seemed that the handle of the barrow had slipped from their hands and now I was on my own, gaining speed, and surely headed into a collision course with the cement banking topped with a barbed fence. On the other side of it lay a daunting abyss filled with god-knows-what-all-I-do-not-want-to-even-know.

As was destined, a few seconds later, the barrow collided

with the barbed fence, and off flew the barrow to the other side of the fence with its sole occupant me, the lone passenger on the flight. In those few seconds when I was airborne I was certain that a chapter of my life had ended, and I hoped and prayed it wouldn't be the last one. In that flight, I shut my eyes tightly and thought of my siblings and my parents, I thought of my fellow boarders, many friends including the ones back home in the plains below. I even thought of, I still wonder why, the barking face of the Sports Captain… as the perilous flight of the wheelbarrow over the fence made its way towards the abyss in the mountain.

Eventually, the flight landed, and I tell you the landing was not smooth at all. The uneven surface of the rocky landing made the barrow topple and turn on to the left side, while I, the passenger, was tossed on to the right side. It is hard to say where the barrow disappeared in the abyss but my fall was stalled by a labyrinth mesh of 'Girardinia diversifolia[1]' commonly known as '*bichchu-buti*'. Need I say what became of me thereafter!

With extreme caution, I painfully managed to crawl out of the 'Girardinia diversifolia' abyss, itching and scratching all the way for an hour long upwards haul. I reached the

---

1. *a herbaceous plant, which has jagged leaves covered with stinging hairs.*

valley, still scratching my back and legs vigorously, but I couldn't tell anyone what had happened. Mr. Shukla, Headmaster of the Boys' School, noticed the scratching me and advised I must immediately visit the hospital. He went on a discourse on my condition and counseled me about an unusual allergic reaction often caused when tender skin is exposed to limestone dust. He called out to the two boys nearby who were laying the white lime track marks on the field. As fate would have it, I was reunited with Pippy and Zahir! They kept their eyes down, partially terrified of Mr. Shukla and partially in anticipation that I would rat them out. They obediently carried me to the hospital - not a word was spoken among us about anything but everything was understood in the shared silence.

I was hospitalized for the next two days and was discharged when the swelling - because of the stings of the 'bichchu-buti' - subsided. I did not utter a word to the doctor or to the nurses. I did not even whisper anything to the hospital dog as it sat besides me, looking at me with its enquiring eyes. When the doctor pressed me hard, I told him that the swelling must have been because of an allergy from something I must have had for breakfast. He smirked and wrote a prescription mockingly.

On returning to the hostel late that evening, the House-Captain came to check on me and my health. My bed was sandwiched between Zahir's and Pippy's. I saw that they were awake but were pretending to be asleep. In between the niceties, the House-Captain asked me nonchalantly if I knew anything about the missing wheelbarrow.

I looked up at the roof of the dormitory for a while. Then, I looked at my immediate neighbours who had now pulled their sheets up to cover their faces. Finally, I locked eyes with the House-Captain and replied inquiringly, "What's a wheelbarrow? I have no clue."

THE SCREAM

~ Nitin Dubey

Life in a boarding school is rife with memorable incidents. Sometimes, these incidents are comical, and at other times, these border on the supernatural.

Occasionally, it's both, in a 'Golmaal'[1] meets 'The Conjuring'[2] kind of way.

On the hilly terrain where Oak Grove School is located, at a lower and neglected corner was a cottage surrounded by a well-manicured garden. Occupied by the young Bhanu Pant, our Geography teacher, it had the notoriety of being haunted by the ghost of an ex-teacher who supposedly had committed suicide in the cottage several decades earlier.

---

1. *A popular Indian comedy film*
2. *A popular English horror film*

Bhanu, the young restless professor, had the reputation of being a prankster too. He would never miss an opportunity to fuel an urban legend like this. Therefore, he used to invite small groups of students to his garden well past sunset and entertain them with stories about the dead teacher and the spirit that haunted the cottage. As proof, he would stand on the porch and pretend to channelise his energy by turning off all lights and reciting some mantras, which he affirmed were essential for communicating with the dead spirit. He'd start swaying from side to side, and after a few dramatic moments of pretentious disbelief, speaking in a muffled voice and moaning about his death. Then, suddenly, there would be a piercing banshee scream that startled the naive and immersed audience - the scream sure was unbelievably spooky!

Teacher Bhanu did a pretty good job of enacting this act, getting better with practice with each rendition. Many in the school believed his narration to be truer than true, especially since the naive audience consisted of little children, most of whom were believers in the supernatural. The whole act by teacher Bhanu used to be a long one, and most children used to run away out of fear before he would break out of character.

One evening after dinner, I along with two of my batchmates went to the garden to have a first-hand experience of what the hullabaloo was all about. That night too Bhanu executed his well-rehearsed act flawlessly in the pitch dark moonless night. Although I knew it was an act, it sowed doubt in my mind, "What if this is for real!" In between that moment of contemplation, one of my batchmates got spooked beyond his wits and started to run back to the hostel. Almost instinctively, and perhaps because of the fear and doubts playing on our minds, I along with the other batchmate also started to run towards the boys' hostel.

We hastened, breaking into a sprint, crossed the squash court, and doubled up the stairs in front of the auditorium, joined into the driveway to the boys' hostel, all the while running and screaming 'Ghost! Ghost!'. It seems silly now but back then it was what made our minds freak with fear or fun, or a mix of both.

As we were running towards the safer harbour, we ran into Mr. Bhatt (Economics teacher and my housemaster), Mr. Pande (Maths teacher), and Mr. D. C. Pant (our headmaster who was also related to Bhanu). Seemingly, the trio was out for a stroll after their evening supper.

They noticed us and were curious about our state of undue excitement. Mr. Bhatt called out loud and commanded us to stop. He enquired with authority why, where from, and from whom we were running away.

Out of breath and nerves, we wondered how to respond or to explain our tomfoolery. Added to our dilemma was the possibility of getting punished for being out of the hostel without permission, so I blurted out the first thing, probably also the truth, that came to my mind. "We saw a GHOST!" One of my batchmates joined in the attempt to save our sinking boat and exclaimed. "A real ghost near the squash court!"

"What?", said Mr. Pande. "You fools! There isn't a thing like that! Show us this Ghost of yours!"

Caught in a tricky situation, we sheepishly back-traced our run, this time with the trio - Mr. Bhatt, Mr. Pande, and Mr. Pant, down the driveway, downwards the stairs, and across the squash court, to the notorious cottage.

When we got closer, but not close enough to reach the cottage yet, we heard a piercing soul-stirring banshee scream again. It was coming from the thick darkness ahead of us. From a distance, the echo of the hilly surroundings and the white mist slowly seeping in made the high-pitched scream sound like an exorcism gone awfully wrong!

All of us - the children and the elders - looked at each other, our eyes dilated and our foreheads contracted. Looking back today, I know what was going on - Bhanu was terrorising the next lot of students who had arrived after we had left!

Mr. Bhatt was the first to speak. "Let's disperse today and enquire about the unusual sound when the day breaks tomorrow." Mr. Pant and Mr. Pande quickly added a series of yes-es to Mr. Bhatt's wise counsel. Seizing the opportunity, we, the little children of Oak Grove, ran back to the boys' hostel, laughing, screaming, and joyous about the two narrow escapes we had that dark night.

To this date, I don't know what the teachers made of the screams, but I imagine that they too must have made a quick exit to save their lives, scrambling and scuttling back to their dens in an attempt to avoid a rendezvous with the spirit of Oak Grove!

THE DAMN DICTATION

~ Sudip Bajpai

On 15th August 1985, my father sent the school rickshaw away as I waited in suspense inside the family bathroom. I was overcome with joy and overwhelmed with emotion. How could a father be so considerate? Over the next 30 minutes, I understood that I had not understood. On that particular Independence Day, I went through what the freedom fighters must have suffered at the hands of the British. With my well oiled hair horribly out of place, my half-pant refusing to hold my shirt, and my tie losing its sense of position, I spent the rest of the day standing outside our railways quarters in Lucknow. I had been met with what is called corporal punishment. It was not sudden. It had been coming for some time as under the massively able guidance of my grandfather, I had learnt to hide in the bathroom at the appropriate moment, the moment when the school rickshaw arrived. There is this affection of grandparents that spoils a kid. It is as if they are avenging their child by treating their child's child as if he were the last incarnation of God Vishnu, or may be when one becomes an octogenarian, one starts to understand the futility of pressure, competition, anger etc. much better and tries to find peace in the innocence of grandchildren. My father, who was decades away from becoming a grandfather, had different views. And so, fittingly, I lost all my fear of school as I was exposed to the more violent fear of my father's robust hand meeting me, not halfway but well inside my territory.

My parents mistook it for enthusiasm and one fine evening Papa said "*Tumko Dada (elder brother) ke school mein daal dete hain.*" ("*You are going to be sent to your elder brother's school.*")

So in the winter of 1986, I found myself seated in a not-so-bright room facing two never-seen-that-tall-before ladies and one oh-he-is-so-short man. We exchanged usual pleasantries and then they got on my case. They wanted to know my name, which I blurted out before the man could reach the question mark. Next in line was "Who is Pradip Bajpai?" Boy this is going good! Then the man muttered something in English, which was rather scary for me to comprehend. I looked to my left or was it right to get some hint from my father. Unfortunately, he had chosen that particular moment to silently admire the curtains. Then I invoked my magical power of 'I don't know.' After quite a few minutes of trying to decipher my various tones of 'I don't know,' the man in the middle asked me in Hindi "*Beta, English samajh mein aati hai?*" (*Son, do you understand English?*), and I replied in English "No sir". Immediately, my father and I found ourselves out of the room.

In the summer of 1986, I was busy dipping my tiny self in the village pond at my grandparents' village villa when I heard somebody calling out my name. Apparently, I had gotten through the admission test and Papa had come to pick me up.

Now in the monsoon of 1986, I unleashed my raw talent on a rather unsuspecting institution set up by the British in 1888 in the hills of Mussoorie to convert raw material like me into a finished good – all glitter and value. There was just one hurdle – The English Language. It wasn't alien to me, it was just not there.

And then there was the English etiquette. Up until that age, I had blindly trusted my right hand to serve me well while eating rice and now I was supposed to use a spoon in tandem with a steel fork. Having meals became a battle against food with weapons like spoon and fork and knife.

Fortunately, my batch found a savior in a classmate who had a year's experience as for some reason she had made herself eligible to stay in the same class for the second year running. We felt that she must have felt bad about it but then she may have had that 'Nadal attitude' of not defending one but adding one more Grand Slam to the tally – hers was Class III. She was well versed with the corridors and could safely guide a boy to his reserved place to take a leak if he was mistakenly heading towards the girls' restroom.

Owing to the absence of a class teacher, who was on medical leave even before meeting us, this class of kids found an apt analogy in a fleet of rudderless ships banging against one another and sometimes against the abstract. Then one day, lightning struck. The class teacher surfaced. She was tall, fair, sharp featured and would have been quite a sight in her heydays. Unfortunately, for me and my angelic mates she was not only way but a highway past her heydays and wasn't too happy about that either.

Gloom set in. The back-stabbings among the little ones obliterated faith when one angel would complain against the other reporting even the most minute act of non-compliance to the teacher. Smart boys of the class smarting under the dictatorship of their first official mentor soon figured out ways to bring fun back to class. For one, letting the desk's top fall oh-so-unintentionally that created a Big Bang so as to create a black hole in the teacher's head gave them a constitutional right to get up, say sorry, and move out of the class – they loved it and held a firm belief that the teacher loved it too since they were no more visible to her.

Tough luck though, corridors did not have much activity and there was always a larger danger of the headmistress loitering around. Now, Big Ma'am was tall, imposing, had quite a rough voice for a slender lady with beautiful hair, considered smiling as an unwanted gesture, and spoke only English. Talking or rather answering to her was like a mini civil services interview – name, fame, and reason – and immediate result and posting – a well-oiled cane that could make even the most hardened criminals confess to crimes that they had not even thought of committing. No wonder, I never let the desk fall down even if it meant putting my head in between the top and the base.

Life for me was quiet as I had this gift of going unnoticed day in and day out. In my little head, I would feel insecure when the teachers would praise someone or when a classmate got noticed for some endeavor of hers or his. Forty five days in the hills, I still preferred the scorching heat of my grandmother's village and that muddy pond.

On a wonderfully bright morning, the teacher instructed us all to get ready for "ENGLISH DICTATION" – her idea of pay-back. I was still struggling with English when this new term 'dictation' banged the door down and entered my space. With retreat or running away not being viable options, I surrendered myself to the mercy of Almighty though the halo with horns that seemed to glow just behind the teacher's head.

My classmates explained to me that dictation was the process of writing down the spelling of the words that the teacher would speak. Out of their affection for me, rascals forgot to tell me that the spellings had to be right too. My copy came back covered in red wine and I was noticed, or you can say discovered, for my achievement, which was scoring a pair. Our teacher took great pride in putting two zeroes where she could have been miserly and used one. Somehow, after every dictation, I felt I had done well. In my mind, the spellings could have no other combination or sequence of letters. Oxford dictionary was never on the same page, nor was Bhargava's[1].

Having tasted blood, the teacher went for the kill now and ordered, all who could have heard her, the dates for the monthly test. The monthly test is a version of the mundane impromptu test, but a thousand times more lethal, because the results flow through to the Headmistress on the way to our Parents. I heard her announcement with some trepidation.

This time when the results were announced, I stood 5th in my section of around 30 kids. I stood 5th, again, with a golden pair. Had the world agreed to use the spellings invented by me, 'histree kood have bean krietedd'. The headlines would have been scorching. Some unknown

---

1. *a popular English to Hindi Dictionary providing correct standard pronunciations and ascents in Hindi.*

unseeded player who did not even understand the term dictation, let alone the process, might have just topped the class. Oak Grove School denied its indigenous Boris Becker. For the uninitiated, Becker won the Wimbledon title at the age of 17 in the year 1985 as an unseeded boy.

What followed for me, unfortunately, was anonymity and the a-date-in-court experience of dictation every week. Are you looking for a girl in my life who came and lifted me from the depths of anonymity to great heights? If yes, forget it. History and lady luck both eluded me not by a centimeter or an inch but by a pair.

1987 was a different year. I fell in love with Ms. Sahni, my new class teacher, and supposedly she was also head-over-heels for me. To prove her love, she gifted Spell-Well to me and asked me to mug up all the words before I could go back to play time in the flats. Love is cruel – may be not as cruel as the Damn Dictation, though!

THE HOUSE OF CARDS
~ Vikas Chandra

Part 1: The Premise
"There's no friends like the old friends"
- James Joyce

Speaking of lasting friendships, there can't be any firmer ones than those formed in the formative years in a boarding school. My association with Deepak Mohanty, who is a batch senior to me, is one such friendship. The stories about our unique experiences at school have entertained many at family get-togethers and friendly reunions. Recently while I was visiting Mohanty's place, his wife and daughters, at an opportune moment, insisted on sharing a leaf from our boarding school days.

Deepak, a friend and a senior to me, had always been a topper in academics. A rare person, who loved studying and had a passion for academics, he was perceived as a studious and boring senior by my batch. No one messed with him since he was genuinely considered to be a no-nonsense person. Although now, around twenty years later, he has transformed and has also developed a good sense of humour. I credit this transformation, in good humour, to the many romantic heartbreaks he has been through in his life.

The heartbreaking incidents are not about adolescence or teenage ones but something much more childlike and innocent. The junior school days were the most tender years of our time in the boarding school. Small and frail students from Class 3 to Class 5 lived together in the harsh yet beautiful terrain of the Himalayas. During the cold days, most of our time was spent in the dormitory. I fondly remember sleeping in the Victorian style large dormitory hall with hundred plus beds, all neatly arranged in rows and columns.

Discipline is another common term in a boarding school. It's a denomination that may also denote a tug-of-war between teachers and students. But ask any person who has studied in a boarding school, all good nostalgic memories are born out of this unsophisticated tug-of-war. In junior school, since the students were much younger, this tug of war was mostly won by the teachers. Led by a strict martinet of a headmistress, the teacher's team easily routed the children in the game.

Also, the word 'caning' was enough to scare any kid towards discipline. Whenever we indulged in an act of indiscipline, the headmistress would summon her richly oiled cane and smack our tender bottoms or the back of our thighs in front of everyone in the school. The same 'caning' was a badge of honour when we moved on to Senior School (Class 6 to Class 12). Being 'caned' was a sort of yardstick to measure who would play better in the senior tug of war of indiscipline. The student who was caned the highest number of times in junior school was treated with the utmost respect in the senior school.

Part 2: The Story

"There is a certain part of all of us that lives outside of time. Perhaps we become aware of our age only at exceptional moments and most of the time we are ageless."
– Milan Kundera

We were in the fourth standard when four of us classmates had developed this childish notion of being more mature than the rest of the other mates. We got excited after having sneaked in a pack of playing cards to the dormitory. We did not know how to play, however, having possession of such an adult accessory was exciting and gave us a sense of superiority over others. Nicholas Sparks was right when he wrote that people want pretty much the same things: they want to be happy. Most young people seem to think that these happy things are somewhere in the future, while older people believe their happiest moment lies in the past.

We, four of us, decided that the most opportune time to play cards would be when everyone was asleep and after our strict headmistress would have completed her customary stroll in the dormitory to check and confirm that all have slept. As per our plan, the headmistress left the dorm and we all got out of our beds, thus ending our pretence of sleep. When we reached the lighted spot in the alley, we realized that we were not the only ones and that there was another person who was up to utilize the silent hours under the only lighted night bulb. We sat on the ground and started piling on the cards to build our respective houses of cards. The fifth boarder had taken a book from under his pillow to study. Being the first night, we played quietly. However, we gradually learned the play of the night and enjoyed stacking our cards. It took around ten nights for us to become proficient and our cards started stacking up to the fourth level. We were carefree, at times overconfident, and would jokingly declare ourselves to be the night kings of the dormitory.

On that day, the studious fifth person came to counsel us not to make noise. We brushed his counsel aside and instead asked him to join us to build his own house of cards. He got upset and was visibly agitated. He threatened to complain to the headmistress if we wouldn't stay quiet. We rebutted and threatened him too. We reminded him that studying under the lamp during sleeping hours was also not allowed. We added that if he ratted on us, we would also drag him down along with us.

The next day, we were quite sure that he would not complain about us, as he was also committing an act of indiscipline, albeit a less severe one than the one we were doing. We assured ourselves that he was too cowardly to complain about us. So, the next night, four of us woke up and sat under the night bulb again, to build our house of cards. We gleefully clapped when each level got completed, sometimes loudly and purposefully with the intent of disturbing and teasing the fifth boarder.

The next day, the headmistress came for her usual rounds and we five as usual were faking as if we were asleep. As the headmistress came near our section, we saw our studious boarder getting up from his bed. I was not sure what went on in other's heads, but I was pretty confident of the trouble ahead; our house of cards had fallen even without being built. I saw him pointing to our beds and gesturing in detail about how four of us played cards and made noises that did not let others sleep. We were called for and asked to be woken up by the sturdy dormitory staff. We tried our best to act as if we were deep in sleep, but with our poor acting and with a few tight slaps, we gave in.

We were asked by our headmistress to step out of the dormitory for an inquiry about the cards. We got into our dressing gowns and stepped out. The headmistress and her staff were followed by the studious guy. Trailing them were the four culprits. The headmistress instructed her staff to bring the famous cane out for the four of us. When the staff left to bring the cane, I immediately raised my hand and pointed to the studious boarder, and said to the headmistress, "Ma'am, we four admit to being guilty of playing cards, a game we did not know a few days back, until he taught us." The studious boarder was aghast. I continued, "He used to play with us as well. But yesterday he lost to us when our houses were taller than his. Ma'am, we acknowledge that we teased him for losing the game. He is snitching on us for revenge. He deserves to be punished more than us."

Immediately the other three joined the chorus and nodded at my logic of the vindictive, scheming, studious evil among us. I felt victorious at the inability and shyness of the studious guy to ably defend himself.

That long night, the headmistress exercised her wrist with fury, and caned all five of us.

Part 3: The Finale

"In the sweetness of friendship let there be
laughter, and sharing of pleasures.
For in the dew of little things the heart finds
its morning and is refreshed."
– Kahlil Gibran

As I narrated this tragic yet humorous story of yesteryears to Deepak's daughters, there was a persistent smile on Deepak's face. When his daughters left us alone, Deepak said with a hearthy laugh, "Why are you shaming me in front of my wife and daughters? The four of you were devils back then when you lied shamelessly to Ma'am."

The daughters joined the two of us along the story and lauded all the fun we had in our hostel days. The elder one turned to her father and in good humour rebuked him for playing cards and for framing the studious boarder on false charges. Deepak looked at me and smiled as he patted her daughter.

That evening was full of nostalgia where we narrated our hostel stories to the young girls. Deepak became sentimental and took out a diary he had preserved since his childhood. It was our school notebook with the Oak Grove emblem printed on it. In the diary, he showed us the love letters he had drafted for his classmates who would then rewrite the letters in their own handwriting and share it with their girlfriends in the Girls' School across the valley. Deepak's letters were lovingly written and sensitive in nature. We wondered if the girls ever realised that it was not their boyfriend's thoughts they were reading but Deepak's.

Deepak's wife promptly acknowledged that the thoughtful letters by Deepak were instrumental in her being attracted to him. The children had a glow of pride in their eyes for their lovely father.

Boarding school students are a rare breed. They are a unique combination of contemporary, old but strong school traditions and culture. Children of boarding schools treasure friendships. In the era of fragile relationships, the foundations laid in boarding schools build robust relationships within the society.

RICE SHOUP
& BATER MUTTON
~ Raghu Menon

Raja Baksh and his tuck box with those pulling sweets and pastries... As a junior school student, I was sure that his name was Raja Box, not Baksh; the other boarders in Oak Grove School, the residential school where I grew up, had got it all wrong. In any case, all that mattered to us, the ever-ready and always-hungry boys of the boarding school, were his savouries. Away from our parents, we were bound by our friendship and by our love for food - not the kind that we got in the school mess though.

Vacations had started that day and the crowd was gone except for a few of us whose parents made it a routine to come last to pick their wards up, much like the ranks we got in our classes. Harijit, Byomkesh, and I were on the tennis court, serving as the ball boys for the senior boys of the school, the champs in the making, when along came Mr. Box – or Mr. Baksh. As an aside, I called Harijit 'Harya', for no reason really, while Byomkesh was universally called 'Raavan', and for a good reason too. Apparently, during *Dussehra* festivities a few years ago, he had burst into tears as Raavan[1] was set on fire. Back to the main story though. The three of us gathered around Mr. Box, and that was the first time he told us about the *Pahadi* village at Gaimukh and the delicious '*Rice Shoup and Bater Mutton*'. These were supposed to be delicacies from the Queen of the Hills 'Mussoorie'.

Mr. Box then regaled us with another tale. Some two kilometers from the village was a '*mazaar*'[2]. No one ever went there after sunset. In fact, no one went there almost ever. The villagers said, '*wahaan daayan soti hai*' ('*The witch sleeps there*'). Many years ago, some of our seniors had tried to explore the aforementioned *Pahadi* village and had escaped expulsion by the proverbial skin of their teeth. I was petrified by the mention of the *daayan*[*4]. Harya, a

---

1. *as per Hindu mythology, Raavan was the king of Lanka, who Lord Rama slayed*
2. *a Muslim shrine or enshrined tomb*
3. *daayan - witch*

sturdy Surd, acted like a stud, and Raavan, usually the most practical of the lot, decided that he was to guide us on our trip to the village.

Once the school reopened, the story of the *Pahadi* village took over our imagination. The story became a regular feature in late-night dormitory tales. I personally narrated seven or eight versions, all of which were lapped up by my fellow boarders with much relish. Our intent to explore the village grew. Whatever little hesitation we had was easily overcome once we read a couple of Famous Fives and Hardy Boys.

Our first step was getting ourselves admitted to the school infirmary. Sister Stella tucked each of us in for our afternoon nap. As soon as she left, we put pillows under our blankets and snuck out and headed for the village. The only direction that Mr. Box had given us was that we were to walk towards the smoke, and that was what we did. This meant walking through a grove of thick trees, which for the lack of a better word, I will call a dense forest. As we proceeded, the forest got denser and darker, and some sounds that we could hear were definitely not familiar. Harya was leading our pack, Raavan, as his role demanded, was guiding us while I, being too lazy for my own good, was aimlessly following them. Suddenly, I heard a sharp chirping noise. '*Langurs!*' I screamed in horror and started running back towards the school and into the comfort of the infirmary bed. I did not even care to look back. My partners-in-crime followed suit, I learned later. When Sister Stella woke me up for my evening snacks, I saw Harya and Raavan step out of their beds too. There was a common expression of indignation on all our faces, rightful or not, that said '*dagabaaz saaley*'[5].

As we got older, the story of the *Pahadi* village with its '*mazaar*' and '*Rice Shoup and Bater Mutton*' kept gaining strength. By the time we were in the final year, no one really remembered where the story (or may I say stories?) even originated.

I remember it was the last day of school. Now that we were old enough, our parents had permitted us to travel back home independently on our own. This for us was the perfect opportunity, and possibly our last too, to explore the village. So, we set off on the expedition. We walked the same dark and dense forest but this time there were no *langurs* to dissuade us from continuing our adventure.

---

5. *dagabaaz saaley - a slang for turncoat in the Hindi language*

We entered the *Pahadi* village. It smelled a little strange but the thought of the 'Rice shoup and Bater mutton', which had only gotten tastier in our heads over the years, kept us going. There were no shops that we could see, so we pegged on a house that had Rice *Shoup* ready, but the *Bater* Mutton would take some time. Being hungry, as we were, we decided to have the Rice *Shoup*, visit the *mazaar* and then come back for the *Bater* mutton. We asked for three bowls of the Rice *Shoup*. It cost a princely ten rupees. We gulped it down and headed for the *daayan* abode at the *mazaar*.

As we got closer to the *mazaar*, Harya announced that the Rice *Shoup* had *bhang* in it, for sure. I, almost instantly, agreed and believed that it had started working already. The *mazaar's* compound was deserted and gloomy. There were some large, ominous-looking trees and plants. I believe I even heard some weird voices. I sneaked a look at my watch. We needed to get out of that place before six. I had never met a *daayan* to date and had no intention of changing that status. However, we hadn't found the *mazaar* yet. We looked around for a while before we found a heap of soil in the corner with weeds and mushrooms growing on it. Creeped out, as we were, and with the Rice *Shoup's* effect getting stronger, we started to claw away at the soil.

In some time, we found a large stone slab – about 10 feet by 15 feet. We looked for some Arabic inscriptions that would tell us that the slab we had found was the tombstone. Our history lessons had taught us that *mazaars* have holy words engraved on them. This *mazaar* had nothing on it!

It was getting dark. We lit a bonfire, thanks to Raavan's lighter, to help us see. I had carried a torchlight which also came in handy. After careful inspection we did find '*Robinson Dorothy Benedict – 1827*' inscribed on the stone. This was a Britisher's grave, not a Muslim's *mazaar*!

By then, the Rice *Shoup's effect* had peaked. Raavan announced that we should shift the stone slab. Even in my state of intoxication, or perhaps because of it, I discouraged the idea vehemently. Harya quickly leapt to the slab to help in Raavan's mission. The Punjabi strength was on display, or maybe the slab itself was loose in the first place; in any case, the slab was moved. We could see a deep, rectangular pit. Harya flashed his torchlight into it.

Aah! Harya screamed and fell back. He started running and, seeing him, Raavan started to run too, banging his head hard on a tree. His head was now bleeding profusely but we did not stop. I, like a lemur, ran behind them with all the strength I had. We ran for what felt like a long time. The *Pahadi Bater* Mutton, that we had looked forward to eating since the day Mr. Box had told us about it, was forgotten in the frenzy. We stopped only once when we were near the Dehradun railway station. Harya was shivering; he had seen a woman in the pit with her eyes wide open, he said. Raavan and I went weak on our knees and almost fainted!

Years passed, the three of us remained friends and interacted as often as our busy lives allowed us to. We were part of several alumni platforms and attended reunions together. We were also part of a few in-group skirmishes. However, there was one unsaid golden rule that we followed – we never spoke about our rendezvous with the wide-eyed woman, six feet under, in the *Pahadi* village.

30 years passed by. I was in Perth when I got a call from Raavan. Harya was in Mussoorie and both Raavan and I needed to meet him there the very next day. It was urgent. I flew down to India and met Raavan and Harya in Barlowganj - a place close to Jharipani where Oak Grove School has stood since 1888 . Harya had something to share.

Harya had been living in the UK for some years now. On a visit to Manchester, he had come across a restaurant that served '*Rice Soup and Bater Meat*'. It was the most popular item on the menu and had been so for the last three generations of the restaurant. The recipe seemingly was a family secret. The restaurant was started by a gentleman called '*Robinson Dorothy Benedict*' – a general in the British Army posted in Chile who had never set foot in India. The dish was an old Latin American dish that originally contained a little opium.

We were dumbfounded by this discovery, or was it just a coincidence? We walked across to the village to find out what we could. An old man, after much persuasion, agreed to speak about it. "The *mazaar* is indeed haunted, *saheb*. Some years ago, three boys tried to open the grave and were swallowed by the *daayan*. I, myself, saw the blood on the ground, splattered on a tree trunk, the dislodged tombstone, and an empty grave."

Whose *mazaar* was it? How did Robinson Dorothy Benedict's name appear on the grave when he had never visited India? Why did they say it was a Latin dish? Did Harya really see the lady in the grave, or had he imagined it all? Harya continues to research on the subject. Raavan, as usual, provides intellectual support, and I continue to be the catalyst.

THE DAY THAT WAS
~ *Mangu Srinivas*

For the boarding school boys, Sports is not just another drill. It is the elixir of their being - a means to make a statement of their prowess, and a channel to express the honour of their institute. Indeed, for us - the children of Oak Grove School, sports was thus and much more than that.

I vividly remember to this day, the finals of the Inter-School Cricket Tournament played over three decades ago, between Oak Grove School, an institution I am part and proud of, and St. George's College, our befitting arch-rivals and an equally amazing institution.

Here is what happened between these two schools, one fine

sunny day, over thirty years ago.

The crowd was getting thick and already in a frenzy. It was as if the entire Garhwal Hills had gathered to witness the event of the year. The school ground was filled with an audience of over 1,500 fervent enthusiasts, all of whom were swelling in excitement. In parallel, a similar crowd of eager viewers sat on branches of the trees at the periphery of the ground beyond the seating arrangements. The whole of Mussoorie had come to a standstill to witness the historic finals of the Inter-School Cricket Tournament between the strongest teams of the two most respectable and reputed schools of Mussoorie. The winner shall be the champions for the next year and will see the name of their alma-mater engraved boldly on the golden trophy.

The Oakgrovians were at the crease and the Manorites were guarding the field. All that was required by the Oakgrovians was 25 runs from the last 18 deliveries to get to the magic figure of 168. The scoreboard was moving slowly but the overs were depleting rather fast. The Manorites[1] had put up a fighting total even after a batting collapse at the beginning of their innings. Their Middle and lower order batsmen played

---

1. *St. George's College (Mussoorie) was founded in 1853 by the Capuchin Fathers and entrusted to the Society of the Brothers of St. Patrick (Ireland) in 1894. It was opened in a cottage known as Manor House; the name by which the campus is still known. The students are known as Manorites.*

some splendid shots towards the end of their 25 overs limit.

Khaled took the first stride in his run-up as the crowd roared. On the other end of the pitch, Arjun was holding the Oakgrovian batting together and stayed solid since early afternoon. His persistent determination showed in the 29 runs flashing against his name on the scoreboard. The cheering Oakgrovians had put their faith in him and the whole school was looking up to Arjun to show his prowess. Many in the crowd pondered, "Will he be able to deliver?"

Khaled, known to be a devastating pace bowler, had an instinct to bowl in the right areas and get wickets. As he closed in on the stumps, the crowd fell silent in anticipation. Arjun from the runner's end watched Mayur who faced the ball. The Manorites were not giving in to Mayur who gave the much-required support and made the wickets stop from tumbling. The ball was pitched up towards Mayur. He took a stride forward and brought his bat in line with the ball. The ball went straight to the fielder. No Run. The next delivery from Khaled was a straighter one and Mayur pushed it towards the third man for a cheeky single and passed the strike to Arjun.

Khaled had been running hard to generate pace and bounce. The ball was pitched short and Arjun transferred his weight to the back foot and hooked up in the air. The crowd roared in excitement. The ball crossed the boundary line. His score moved up to 33. This was his highest score against the Manorites. Even though his performances against other teams were much better, he could never score against the Manorites. He was hoping that that day would be different.

Seeing a boundary hit on his bowl, Khaled's face had cringed. Nishanth, a seasoned player, playing his 3rd Inter-School finals, rushed towards the bowler. "Cool it buddy, you got to keep this bloke out of strike and we have the game." Nishanth realised that winning this game depended on keeping Arjun away from strike. In recent times the Oakgrovians had snatched most of the trophies from the Manorites. St. Georges did not win any major tournament against Oak Grove that year and therefore they desperately wanted to stake a claim on this one.

Khaled hurried towards the stumps for the next delivery of the over. Focusing only on the stumps, he released the ball.

Perfect Yorker.

Arjun gave it all and somehow managed to get his blade behind the ball. The ball strolled towards the leg. "Run!" Arjun shouted at Mayur who lowered his head and darted towards the other end. Together they stole a quick single. The crowd cheered as Mayur safely reached his crease. In the next ball, Mayur hit the ball towards the cover and got a comfortable single. Khaled looked like a charging bull running towards the stumps as he released the next ball. It was pitched outside the off-stump and Arjun guided it square off the wicket.

Two crucial runs were added to Arjun's score.

"Come on, Arjun, don't let it slip out from here", whispered Mr. Kichlu, the legendary Principal of Oak Grove School. Abhay, who sat close to Mr. Kichlu, wanted his younger brother to win the game for Oak Grove.

Arjun had failed to deliver in a few crucial matches earlier and that raised doubts about his capabilities. But that was another game, a different opponent, and the stakes were not this high. Will Arjun be able to deliver or will he succumb again? Abhay's mind was muddy since the time Arjun came to bat.

17 Runs from 12 Deliveries… so read the scoreboard at the far end of the field.

The Manorites huddled towards mid-on. This time Nishanth tossed the ball towards Pravin. Pravin with more than 15 wickets was the most experienced member in the tournament. "This is 'Do or Die' for us. We have done it before and we will do it today", Nishanth spoke to his fellow members in a commanding voice. The team dispersed to take up their positions on the field as Pravin sized his run-up.

"Let's do it, boys! This guy is no match for us", shouted Gautam from behind the stumps creating psychological pressure on Mayur.

Mayur took his place in front of the stumps. Pravin started approaching the stumps. Mayur was ready to face. That was a slower delivery, one of Pravin's trademark. Mayur completely misread it. His bat got into the shot a bit too early and the ball found its way to hit the wickets. Mayur looked back at the wickets and was visibly in shock. The fortress that he was trying to defend had been conquered. The Oak Grove dressing room went silent. The fans of Oak Grove School watched in disbelief.

On the St. Georges side, the celebrations erupted. The Manorites were off their seats, elated and jubilant, and cheered at the top of their voices.

The team members rushed towards Pravin and congratulated him. The veteran had done the trick once again.

"Relax and stay with Arjun till the end", Anil, the Captain of the Oak Grove team, told Sunil, as Sunil reached for his gloves with trembling hands. Sunil nodded nervously and started his walk towards the crease.

"Sunil is the next man in", Nishanth informed his team during the team huddle. Their think-tank analysed each player and formed a strategy to neutralise the opponents. Thanks to their coach who had represented the state in the Ranji Trophy, and had brought in analytics in the game. They studied their opponents and understood the strengths and weaknesses of each player.

"This guy gets nervous when he is attacked around his legs. You know where to attack", Nishanth turned over to Pravin.

The Manorites were meticulous in their approach.

The St. Georges fans started a cheer to acknowledge their wicket-taking bowler. It seemed it was only a matter of time that the year's Cup would be theirs.

Arjun came halfway down the ground to get some extra time to talk to his partner. Both the Oak Grove batsmen walked towards the crease deep in discussion.

"We need a single", whispered Arjun to Sunil.

A charged-up Pravin was ready on his mark as Sunil reached the crease. He took his guard. The Manorites closed up. The pressure was more on Sunil to score a single than on the Manorites who were hovering all around him. They had to consume the remaining deliveries and keep Arjun away from strike.

Sunil brought his bat down at Pravin's next delivery blocking it with a straight bat. The ball went past Pravin. Pravin stretched towards his right but the ball got away from him by a whisker. The Oak Grove batsmen took a quick single.

A confident Pravin prepared his next weapon as Arjun watched patiently. Arjun waited for the ball to come. He went on his back foot and played very late. The ball darted towards the boundary.

"Run!", shouted Arjun as he raced towards the other end. Sunil responded. The fielder at the boundary put every bit of energy chasing the ball. He cut the ball inches from the boundary line, swiftly picked it up, and threw it towards Gautam.

"Come, Come!", shouted Arjun as he turned and ran for a second. Sunil turned and ran as fast as he could. Arjun grounded his bat just in time but that did not stop Gautam from dismantling the bails.

The ground reverberated with cheering St Georges fans applauding their players.

The Manorites were not letting anything pass by them today in the field. With their efforts, they had saved more than 15 runs. Nishanth felt like going and having a word with Pravin. But he restrained himself and thought, "Pravin is a seasoned campaigner and has been in similar situations many times before."

Arjun pushed the next ball towards cover and completed a comfortable single.

Pravin to Sunil…

Pravin relied on his pace as he delivered a faster one. Sunil flicked it towards the leg. One run added to the Oak Grove total. Arjun took his stance. "I should not be predictable", Arjun thought as he opened his stance wider pointing towards mid-on. This change, at this time of the innings, surprised everyone, especially Nishanth. He immediately rushed towards Pravin. "Pravin, this guy is up to something. Bowl at full length. Don't give him room to free his arms."

Pravin had put in some extra effort for the next ball. The ball swung a bit too much towards the Off-side.

"WIDE!" called the umpire. The crowd roared. This time it was the Oakgrovians who were jubilant. The crowd was not just watching 'the Finals' - they were as much participating and playing it!

Cricket had outgrown from the physical sport it used to be, into a psychological sport. Both the teams were trying to put each-other under pressure. Both the matches, the one on the field and the one inside their mind, was getting to their nerves.

Pravin cursed himself. He now realized that he had been taken for a ride. This angered him and his mood showed in the twitch of his eyes. On the next delivery, he came back with a vengeance. Arjun, having nudged the ball towards gully, called and ran. Sunil followed his cue and rushed to get to the safety of the crease on the other side. A fielder, who was positioned there for such shots, took a step and stopped the ball with an amazing dive. He had stopped a definite boundary, but couldn't stop the scorers as they added another run to Oak Grove's total.

End of Over.

The atmosphere on the ground had turned electric in the last couple of overs.

In the stand, Principal Kichlu moved uneasily in his seat. Abhay, seated close to the dignitaries, was silent for the last half an hour. It seemed that he had even forgotten to blink. 10 runs were required off the last 6 deliveries.

Arjun managed to retain the strike and was ready for the final 6 deliveries. "Hold your end. You are doing it very well. We will get there," Arjun told Sunil pointing towards the prized Cup on the pedestal in the ground. They started to walk towards their creases. The pressure to face these final six deliveries was more than he had faced in his entire life.

Nishanth summoned Krishnan, their bowling spearhead, whose bowling figures read as Overs-4 / Maiden-1 / Runs-16 / Wickets-2. Krishnan was considered as one of the best spin bowlers in the district. His Midas touch during the previous matches showed his form during the season. His spin bowling had turned out to be lethal on the dry pitch that day. Nishanth, an intelligent Captain, had saved his precious wicket-taking bowler for the final over.

Arjun took his stance. Krishnan started his short run-up. Krishnan lofted the ball in the air to allow it the time to spin as he would have desired. Arjun took a long stride forward and worked the ball in the gap towards cover. Single.

Sunil took guard. Krishnan smartly took an extra minute before bowling which allowed the crowd to settle down and forced the batsman to get unsettled. He ran up to the wicket and tossed the ball. Sunil got to the back foot and tried to flick the ball towards the leg boundary. He missed and Krishnan struck. The leg stump lay on the ground. Sunil was dazed and did not know what hit his stumps.

All the eleven players on the field along with the Manorite supporters in the crowd erupted with joy at the same time.

The Oakgrovians fell silent with conspicuous disappointment.

As the new man walked in, the scoreboard showed 9 to win in 4 balls. The Oak Grove tail walked in as Sunil was the last of the recognized batsmen in Oak Grove's team.

"Good going guys, we now have them by their tail. Let's wind it up," Nishanth high-fived Krishnan as the team joined for another huddle.

Rajinder Singh Mann walked in. Arjun approached Rajinder "Take it easy buddy. The last thing we need now is me or you walking back to the dugout. Need to take a single."
"Come on boys, let's send the Oakgrovians packing," Gautam shouted from behind the stumps.

All the Manorite fielders had rounded up the new batsman to make sure he didn't get any gap. Rajinder was so nervous that his forehead showed beads of sweat. He mustered up all his courage and looked towards the umpire. The noise was unbearable as the umpire didn't hear Rajinder's call the first time. "Leg Stump, please!", the new batsman had to shout to be heard.

Krishnan started his run-up. That ball was a faster one and Rajinder just put his bat in time. The ball hit the bat and went wide of the 2nd slip. The batsmen ran for a single. The Oakgrovians in the crowd came alive once again. The task was getting tougher for the Oakgrovians as some of the Oak Grove fans had begun to give-up on their team.

The single brought Arjun back on strike. The scoreboard reflected 8 runs from 3 balls.

Krishnan was ready with the ball. The ball came in flat and gave very little time for Arjun to react. He adjusted his feet and lofted the ball behind the bowler. Krishnan jumped but the ball soared above him. The two batsmen started running towards the other end. Arjun shouted "Two! Two!" as they completed the first one and returned for the second.

At the same time, the fielder collected the ball and threw it towards the keeper in a swift action. The throw was accurate and powerful. Arjun struggled to make ground. This was a race between him and the ball. It was a direct hit.

"HOWZAT!" The call by all the Manorites was so loud that it made a few sparrows fly off from one of the Oak trees. The umpire turned to consult the leg umpire.

All the eyeballs in the ground and the crowd followed the umpires and waited for their decision. If anyone wanted to understand the meaning of "Pin Drop Silence", it was that moment.

The umpires had made their decision and started to walk towards their positions.

"NOT OUT!", declared the main Umpire. The Oakgrovians were still in the game - the Cup reappeared in their wish list.

The crowd roared in excitement. Both teams were giving everything they had. Their preparations were paying off. Indeed, the two best teams in the hills of Mussoorie were clashing, and neither of the teams were prepared to lift the runners-up trophy.

6 Runs 2 Balls.

The umpire took his place behind the stumps. Nishanth stood next to Krishnan as they discussed the next delivery. "We need to get him off the strike. I want him to take a single and not more than that. Let's do it," Nishanth moved to take his position at forward short leg. Krishnan started his run-up. Arjun took his stance. The ball came straight at Arjun. He took a step forward and swung the bat. Arjun anticipated a spin in the ball, but the straight one surprised him. He failed to read the ball and missed. The ball slipped past him towards the wicket-keeper. Gautam stood close to the stumps.

The Oakgrovians held their breath. Their dream to hold the prized cup seemed to be over. They will have to wait for another year.

There are moments where the excitement takes a toll even on the best of the players. Gautam closed his hands a bit too soon and the ball rolled out of his hands. Arjun kissed his glove for luck, thanked the Gods, before regaining control of the crease as any champion would.

The Oakgrovians breathed shallowly with tension.

Krishnan kicked the pitch in his disappointment, tearing the blades of grass. A small chance was all that was required to change the result of this match.

Was that the moment that would see a hero rise to the occasion? Was that the moment that would make a champion stand tall?

Nishanth pulled his cap over his face to hide behind it. He didn't want to expose his feelings to the hundreds of fans.

Last ball to go…

The Manorites were almost on the verge of a historic win. They felt the blood rush in their veins. Last ball to go and Only Arjun separated them from victory.

Arjun had been in a similar situation before. He had failed then. He had let down his team, his coach, and his mates. He could not deliver on that day when they all required him to.

He took his stance and focused hard.

Krishnan started his run-up. He released the ball. He held back his wrist, a trick, to bowl a slower ball.

Arjun sensed the wrist movement and took a step forward. His changed stance helped him to get a high backlift. He heaved towards the pitch of the ball. The bat connected well. The sweet sound of the willow could be heard by everyone on the ground and by the hundreds of eager spectators watching the match.

The ball soared high in the air.

There was a man positioned in the deep as if this shot was anticipated. The Manorites were indeed very thorough with their homework.

They had done complete research on each player of the Oak Grove team, leaving nothing to chance.
The man started running towards the ball and positioned himself to gulp the cherry into his waiting hands.

I do not wish to reveal what happened next. We - the

Oakgrovians, the Manorites, and the spectators - know who lifted the trophy that sunny day over thirty years ago. When I think of that day, I recall clearly the two wonderful teams made of excellent sportsmen. I recall two splendid schools founded on strong values and ethics. In my mind, both the teams won. Both the teams celebrated. Everyone rejoiced in the sportsman's spirit. For the honour of their school, and for the glory of Sports.

———◆———

This story inspired the author to explore the tale further in his debut novel – '101 Not Out'

MUMPS, BIRDS & THE BEES

~ Raveesh Gupta

This story may be skipped by the young, the squeamish, and by the morality brigade, but know well before you skip, that this chapter presents the wisdom that is important for any boarder in a residential school - the enlightenment that dawns when lily-white innocence comes face to face with the truth of the world. For some, this enlightenment happens early, and, more often, for many it's late. In my case, it was early; in fact very early by typical standards.

A boarding school is the worst place for any contagious disease. In March 1995, when I was in boarding school, the chickenpox had spread amok, and hardly anyone was left unaffected. Just about six months later in September 1995, mumps - the malady of swollen necks and boiled food - spread wildly. It ensured at least a month-long siesta in the hospital, which was no reason for any celebration. So everybody tried to avert the dreaded 'mumps', but how long could one run from one's own breath! Once again, half of the school was hospitalized, and familiar faces from the hostel were disappearing quickly. To my disbelief, I woke up one morning feeling a little funny in the neck. Off I ran to the mirror, where further shock awaited me.

My chin had disappeared and my neck was almost twice its normal size. I returned to my bed, slipped between the sheets, and shut my eyes tight, trying to sleep. I hoped this was a nightmare and it will disappear the next morning. It didn't. I, the neck-less mumps-wonder, was soon brought to the notice of the authority. I tried outsmarting by making a lame excuse that I had been punched late last night by a senior fifth standard boy, and the swelling must have resulted from the blow. I wonder how I had thought of such a dumb excuse - seemingly, desperation makes morons out of the brightest (which I like to believe I am). Therefore, once again, I was packed off to the school hospital, and admitted to Ward 'C'.

There were two more from my class who were admitted -
SK and VK. Both of them were from Section A of the class.
I had met SK and VK earlier when we were engrossed in the
recruitment formalities for joining the school. This helped
us be friendly, despite being on opposite sides of bitter strife
some days back. There were four beds in the ward. Three
of the beds in the ward have been accounted for. One bed,
the one on my left, was occupied since some clothes were
untidily strewn over it. We did not meet our 'ward-mate' till
later that evening.

AM looked like the guy next door and did not strike as
somebody to be taken seriously. Nevertheless, God had
destined him to enlighten us three on one great wisdom
of our life - the wisdom that sparks the start of the end of
innocence. Soon after our first meeting, we were assigned
our nicknames for our stay in the ward. SK became Kaalu,
VK became Chinky, and I was Golu.

Our conversations invariably veered towards the usual
tales and jokes. When we were a long way into jokes, AM
suddenly asked us, "Do you know what non-veg jokes are?"
We were fumbled by the new terminology and thus replied
in the negative. He then urged us, "Do you want me to

narrate one?" This time we were excited by the offer and we replied in the affirmative. AM shared the joke, which for obvious reasons, I can't mention in my story today, however, I leave a hint - it was about two frogs, one lady, a spitting serpent, and a raincoat. To be honest, the joke was not really funny but still, it opened a door in our lives.

The ideas that joke formed in our minds had profound implications. Until that point of time, we three (possibly the whole of our class) had a rather childish and innocent explanation for the question most parents were terrified of - "How are babies made?" The most hopeless duffers of the class would explain confidently - "The good God makes the babies in high heaven and sends them hurtling downwards for birth." We, the knowledgeable and scientific elite of the class, would challenge the narration scientifically, "Rubbish! Babies grow in their mothers' bellies after marriage, just like the mangoes fructify in summers."

Children in different parts of the world have different analogies. Many believe in the stories of the stork and the bees. That was quite alright for little children. But AM, the inquisitive and the self-proclaimed messenger of the higher powers, decided all versions told to children needed some honesty. Therefore he set forth to tell us the truth, in the rawness and boldness it must be told. He was also partly upset about us not really getting the punch of his 'non-veg' joke. So he went for us directly. "What are you supposed to do with that thing?", he asked, pointing towards our crotches. We replied innocently- "We relieve ourselves with it." "And…?", he asked. We were silent. We knew of no function to fill in the blank followed by the 'and'.

Thus, in the *gurukul* of the Ward 'C' of the hospital in my boarding school, began our education about the finer details and the fundamentals of human reproduction. We listened to the Guru as sincere disciples should, our eyes and mouths gaping wide and ajar. We went into all the hairy details, each and every one of it - our Guru seemingly was a learned man. We were astonished- "How does this guy know so much?" VK refused to believe him. He said that his parents would never lie to him. He was told by his parents that he was sent hurtling down by God until his parents picked him up and declared him their son. We were appalled by the thought, "Was I too…?" As the AM's version of reproduction spread among the mump-ified children in the hospital, the story gathered traction. Most of the boys now believed in their 'new knowledge'. Like the disciples of wise men before us, we too now were a group of 12 enlightened men.

Enlightened with the new knowledge, we began to see the world in a new light. We began understanding why the men in the films made so much fuss about you-know-what. We started understanding the reason for honeymoons just after marriage. We started understanding the double-entendre jokes common in our soaps and lives. A whole new world view had dawned upon us, and for that everybody felt grateful to AM. Our Guru, as we came to know subsequently, was an academic duffer and an unapologetic scoundrel of his class, but for his knowledge of human body parts and its role on reproduction. For that, we all unanimously considered him our Guru.

A few days later, when we were discharged from the hospital, we brought the 'new knowledge' to the Junior School. We started observing our teachers' rooms, and if any of them had their husbands staying overnight, we propped our ears for any suggestive sounds at night. We even spread the 'new knowledge' to the ignorant masses in our class but realized that very few of them were ready for the enlightenment. We stopped spreading the 'wisdom' when a few of the pioneers, who were hell-bent on their missionary task of sharing the facts, were promptly reported to the authorities.

We, the custodians of the truth, chose to lay low for a few days to avoid being labeled as heretics!

THE ACCIDENTAL GOALKEEPER

~ Prabhat Ranjan

Indians are crazy about cricket but there was a time when hockey enjoyed the same privilege. The first half of the twentieth century is considered to be the golden period of Indian hockey. It was next to impossible to defeat India at that time. My alma-mater, Oak Grove School, had the privilege of producing four gems of hockey who represented India in the national team - Eric Pinniger (1928-32), Richard John Carr (1932), Leslie Charles (1928-32), and the astounding Richard Allen(1928-36), the man who went on to guard the goal post for three consecutive International Olympics conceding only two goals in his career.

I was introduced to hockey in the fourth standard in the

Junior School. A year later when I was in the Senior Boys' School, I made my way into the Sub-Junior team of the school, and later into the Junior team of the school, with regular practice and also by timely providence. I gradually made my mark on the hockey field in the position of 'fullback'.

Hockey was a game in which most schools of Mussoorie and Dehradun excelled. In the loving memory of the late Mr. D. M. Swing, a former Physical Training Instructor and master hockey coach, my school had started the 'D M Swing Memorial Hockey Tournament'. All schools of repute from around Mussoorie and Dehradun participated in this prestigious annual tournament.

I was in the tenth standard when, like each previous year, the tournament was held as scheduled in the month of April. The rules allowed two teams of the hosting-school to participate in the tournament. Therefore, that year, we had two teams - Oak Grove (A) and Oak Grove (B). Team A included the best players in our school. I was selected in Team B instead of Team A. This made me a tad bit sad, nevertheless, what mattered most to me was that I was selected in one of the teams.

That year, there were twelve participating teams. These teams were equally divided into four groups. The top team of each group was to qualify for the two semifinals. Our group had Wynberg Allen, Mussoorie - the previous year's semi-finalists, and Welham Boys, Dehradun, the previous year's runners-up. It seemed obvious that we were intentionally kept in that group as a sacrificial lamb - after all, as hosts, Oak Grove needed to ensure that at least one of the previous year's champ must make it to the semi-finals.

Our first match was scheduled with the Wynberg Allen team on the second day of the tournament. The entire school was there in the stands to cheer for us. We, the Oak Grove 'Team B', were committed to giving a tough fight. Unfortunately, to my sheer disappointment that day, I was not included in the playing eleven and had to sit in the stands.

As I sipped my drink, the match commenced with the referee's shrill whistle piercing our ear-drums. Before we could even warm-up to the game, the ball had hit the wooden plank of our goal with a thunderous bang. I stopped sipping and was aghast! There was a silence of shame all around - the hosts were one goal down within the first minute of the game on home turf! There was an uncomfortable hush in the stands. Somehow, I believe, everyone expected this outcome; after all we were the not-so-good 'Team B'. I jollied myself up by convincing my rambling mind that the 'low expectation' from 'Team B' was but obvious, therefore it was better to focus on the drink in my hand.

Soon, within the next few minutes, another goal stunned us all into deeper silence. What would have been an easy save was gifted away by our keeper to the visiting team. The ball went comfortably through the gap between his pads and kissed the plank of the goal post nimbly, stopping dead on touching the plank of the post, as if to mock us.

The mood of the host-school and its team changed for the worse after that goal. It looked as if the Wynberg Allen team was playing with us - the little boys with their toy hockey sticks, rather than playing the game - the sport of the men with style and stamina.

The first half broke on a score of 3-0. The second half of the game was a bit better for us, with only one more goal added, and the final tally was a humiliating 4-0. Quite an embarrassing defeat it was that day!

The boys in the mess room had a quiet dinner. Later, reluctantly, the team regrouped for a meeting. The goalkeeper was on the receiving end for most of the meeting. After minutes of restraint, the goalkeeper let off steam and backed off by declaring himself unavailable for the next game.

In hindsight, this turned out to be a blessing for me.

I was asked if I could be the goalkeeper for the next game. For someone who was made to sit out as an extra, this was an opportunity to be grabbed with open hands. I agreed to take on the responsibility.

In the next game, we had to face the Welham Boys team. Everyone was so sure of our defeat that no spectators turned up for the match. There I was standing on the ground in the goalkeeper's gear, with not even a single admirer to compliment me. While walking to the post, I banged my stick onto the leg-pads to show that I was no amateur, however in my heart, I was feverishly nervous and scaringly anxious.

The match started on the whistle and as expected the Welham

boys started to dominate the game. A few good moves were made by them, but the hosts outwitted the guests. To our good luck, the Welham boys couldn't capitalize against us. Our boys made a couple of neat attacks however lack of experience and teamwork was evident and our ascent fizzled out. As the first half got over, we managed to keep the score sheet clean at 0-0, somehow.

When the second half of the game commenced, we noticed that the Oakgrovians were trickling in good numbers to cheer for us. This boosted the morale of the Oak Grove team. The silent field was now raucous with cheers, "Light the bullet from the gun, C'mon OG show the fun." The Indie flavour was appended to the sloganeering as the cheering boys changed the lines to "Oakgrovians... *Aaha Aaha!* We like it... *Aaha Aaha!*" The real game was now on.

The whole atmosphere had changed. The team unearthed a perennial source of raw energy. We were now like giants, our chests swelling with pride. Somewhere intoxicated by the cheering, we laxed a bit and one of the Welham boys dribbled past everyone, leaving our defense in tatters, to take a bullet-like shot from inside the circle. The ball whizzed towards me. I was frozen, my eyes dilated behind the helmet as I saw and heard the whistling cannonball heading towards me. The ball hit me on my chest and, believe me, I would have had a heart attack had it not been for the robust chestguard that took the impact and made the ball drop lifeless at my feet.

I returned to reality to a burst of applause from the Oakgrovian stands. They saw a brilliant save by me, but I know the truth - I was just lucky. Everything happened so fast that I could not even duck instinctively, which I would have done to save my soul if I could react - to hell with saving the goal! But God had frozen me that day so that I could attain fame.

While the applause continued, I waved my stick in return to acknowledge the adulation. In that match, by an unexplainable rare combination of enthusiasm and luck, we were able to keep the score 0-0 till the final whistle blew. We just couldn't believe that we managed to play a draw against Welham boys. For Team B, this was more than a win beyond any reason or doubt.

As a token of appreciation, at dinner time, in the mess room, everyone banged their plates with their spoons, to show their support for Oak Grove 'Team B'. Of course, this cacophonous display of appreciation was not acceptable in the mess' rulebook, however, the housekeeper on the floor allowed it wholeheartedly.

Being able to play in the tournament was a big learning for me. I believe our match with the Welham Boys team was a lesson for all of us - the children of Oak Grove. No matter what, we fight. No matter how hard, we face it. No matter whatever, we win.

A TALE OF TWO SCHOOL MASTERS

~ Patrick John Lear Corbett

Mr. Sumption taught the classics in the senior classes. Towards the end of the year he taught Ethics and Civics to the lower standards. It comprised an overview of Greek culture, Roman law, Norse mythology, Scandinavian influence on Britain, origin of common law, ethical and civic behavior. It was riveting stuff sprinkled with philosophy and above all speech was his logos of thought.

He was courting Miss Amstel, Junior School teacher. This act of romance endeared them to the idealist in me. He disliked long hair and, while master on duty during meals, would sneak up behind you, pull your hair and say, "Get your hair cut".

One year, during the school holidays, Miss Amstel died in a tragic train accident. We were all sad to hear the news. I think of them from time to time during nostalgic wanderings. In fact, I thought of him today while reading an article on Socrates. At 70, imprisoned, waiting to drink hemlock, he heard of a man who taught the lyre. "Bring him to me, I want to learn." Socrates' friend said, "You are going to die in 3 days." Socrates replied, "Yes, but I have 3 days to learn." Mr. Sumption would have known that story.

***

Mr. Ahmed (nicknamed Fuzzy) taught Geography. He was a prince among equals: kind, charitable and a gentleman. Fifty years ago, in 1953, I told my buddy Dave D'Lemos, "I'm skipping two classes after breakfast today."
Dave: "Where are you going?"
Me: "To Mussoorie to buy a 78rpm record."
Dave: "You will get into trouble."
Me: "I know, but I've got to buy this record."

Straight through the covered shed, front pitch, lower pitch, past the Principal's house, dip into the valley, jog past Jhids, run, walk, jog to Barlowgunj: I was a natural born runner with a testosterone overload. Do not go through Bala Hissar (named after a place in Afghanistan, from where the British had incarcerated a rebel over here during the Afghan wars), take a left past Skinners and the St. George's reservoir, cut through to Kincraig bus terminal, sharp right, Savoy hotel, clock tower, record shop, make the purchase, head back to school. Cross the road to the Majestic. Check the movie poster. Damn, haven't the time to see this. Gregory Peck, Richard Widmark, 20th Century Fox, Yellow Sky; hike back to Oak Grove.

"Mr. Ahmed wants to see you in the Head Master's office. Mr. Clarke, PT master, saw you leave", were the first words I heard on my return to the hostel. Couldn't Mr. Clarke have chased me? No way, not fast enough!

Why was Mr. Ahmed in charge? Mr. Bellew, the Headmaster, was indisposed. My lucky day!

Mr. Ahmed got to the point, "Come in, shut the door. Why did you do it? You're a nice boy. Your conduct was unbecoming." I told him that the 78 was important.

Mr. Ahmed raised his brows and said, "Sit down."

That was unusual!

He continued, "Let me tell you a story. During the recent school holidays, your father was very kind to me. He is the AST[1] in Lucknow?" I replied politely, "Yes, Sir."

"I was on the platform and your father asked me where I was going", he recounted, "To pray at the Allahabad mosque, I said. He asked me not to use the general compartment and use the officer's saloon in the rear instead. Servants will provide refreshment. He asked me if I will require return service. I said, no thank you, I'm staying with my family in Allahabad."

Mr. Ahmed paused and looked into my eyes, "I have taught in Oak Grove for many years, but no one has shown me such kindness. You have dishonoured your father by this action. Now bend over."

Three of the lightest touches of cane scramed my back.

"Take your record and leave," sighed Mr. Ahmed sadly.

The cane didn't hurt. The fact, that I had dishonoured my father, did!

———◆———

----

1. *Assistant Station Superintendent*

SCHOOL ACROSS THE VALLEY

~ Vani Raj

'I am so screwed!', Arushi confessed to the class. 'It wasn't really my fault', she gushed before their judgemental looks. 'I was just filling the slam book in the library and I swear I was being careful. I even asked a junior to *chivvy*[1] for me.'

'What happened, Arushi?' Bhavya asked, voicing that was on everyone's mind. 'What did you do now?'

You see, Arushi did not really have the best of reputation amongst her classmates. And, when it came to things where the boys were involved, they knew she was bad news. It was not that Arushi was particularly careless but somehow the letters handed over to her, in secret, by her batchmates

---

1. *keep a lookout in Girls' School language*

from the Senior Boys' School, always came to the notice of teachers resulting in their confiscation.

In my boarding school, any interaction between senior girls and senior boys was strictly forbidden, other than at the few social, academic, or cultural events. Even when both the schools, Senior Boys and Senior Girls, wore the badge of the same school, their classes were held separately in buildings separated by a valley in between.

Arushi's batchmates had tried to understand the reason for her frequent tragedies. While it could not have been possible that Arushi was a mole planted by the teachers, everyone suspected that something unusual was going on. The happy twinkle in her eyes, her radiant cherubic expression, the excited bounce in her gait, only made teachers more suspicious.

'It was not my fault and I did not do anything. Trust me, peeps. It was just that Ma'am Dhoundiyal turned up out of nowhere all of a sudden and you know how stealthy she can be. That lady moves like a ghost. I did not notice she was standing behind me. I was drawing hearts around his, my crush's, name when she pulled the book from me.'

Arushi covered her face with her hands as her voice trailed away. Everyone was inquisitive and therefore started babbling all at once. Most of us had already filled the slam book. It contained the names of our crushes, the movies we liked (our preferences were anything but ladylike), and the secret details that only a teenager could share - stupid things if I may add in hindsight, in a book which was supposed to go to one of our classmates across the valley.

Mamta, who had refused to be a part of the whole activity bore the I-told-you-so look as everyone tried to think of a way to sort the mess out before the capture of the slam book became common knowledge and common reading material for all teachers.

Their only hope at that moment lay on the chance that their headmistress, Ma'am Dhoundiyal, had not got to it. She was a lazy teacher when it came to, as stated by her, "such frivolous activities" but they were not sure she would refrain from going through such a goldmine of personal information for long.

'Let's go and apologise to ma'am; ask her for the book back', someone suggested.

'She won't just give it back; we know how she is. If anything, she will read it in front of our parents when they come.'

'How about we steal it?' Someone else suggested and this idea received a more favourable response.

'But how do we go about it? We can't sneak in her office at night, it's locked, and the guards are there.'

'We will have to do it during the day then. We don't have much choice.'

'Peeps, I think we will have to do it today', Arushi suggested, confident as now she was again a part of the conversation and no one was blaming her.

Mamta scoffed from her seat. 'Gosh! I did tell you guys so. And since you all are going to be stupid enough to steal it and do it today, why not let Arushi do it.'

'No! I will not do anything like that. I will mess it up again. And besides, you are blessed with such foresight, why don't you do it?' Arushi answered, her temper rising. She was tired of Mamta playing holier than thou for too long.

'Bhavya can do it. She is a favourite with the teachers. Even if someone catches her, she will be able to get away with it easily. She has a good reputation.'

It was Bhavya's turn to get angry now. 'And how do you think I have maintained that good reputation? By not doing such things, of course.'

'Yes, but you have also written in that slam book, remember?'

'I can tell them I did so under peer pressure, and I am sorry', countered Bhavya.

'I will do it', Anjali who had been a silent spectator so far rose from her seat. 'We need to steal that book and send it back to Boys' school. Arushi will help me with it because it's her fault we are even discussing this.'

She laid out a plan. It was simple: draw the teachers away from the staff room and office so that the way is clear while the two of them sneak inside and get the book.

A few shrugged in agreement. Others didn't look that persuaded and were convinced the plan was going to get us in more trouble than anything else. But they were all up for helping their friends do what was necessary, not because a lot of them would have been in trouble over that stupid bundle of papers but because they knew they had to stand by each other. Staying in a hostel had taught them that their family and priority were their friends and classmates; even if they fought or didn't agree with each other, they would stand by them through everything.

***

'Ananya is puking, she is very sick. Please help!' Bhavya ran into the staff room, crying. A few teachers ran out to help her friend who was prostrated in the washroom. They tried to rouse her but Ananya didn't seem to have any strength left in her to be able to move. Her lips were chalk white and she looked pale.

A few more teachers and students joined them, trying to make the poor girl stand and carry her to the dormitory. Bhavya was crying with anxiety; Ananya was one of her closest friends.

'Go now', she whispered to Arushi and went back to crying

for her dear friend. 'Help her ma'am. I don't know what happened. She looks so frail.'

They were only halfway towards the dormitory when another cry went up. 'Rats, rats', someone shouted and then more voices joined her. Suddenly a lot of kids were screaming and running around.

'Take her upstairs. I will have to see what it is', Miss Tiwari told the other teachers and Bhavya as she ran towards the source of the din. 'What is wrong with these kids!'

When she reached the end of the hall, she saw the whole class X standing on their chairs, screaming. 'RATS! RATS!' More teachers joined her at the source, wondering what was wrong.

'GET DOWN, NOW!' Miss Tiwari raised her voice. She glared at the girls, 'What has gotten into you girls? This is the worst batch ever.'

'I agree with you, Miss Tiwari', joined another teacher. 'We all left the staff room, even the headmistress is here, all because these girls saw some rats. Rats?'

'What are you all, ten? How can you behave like this? And what kind of example are you setting for the junior batches?' The girls hung their heads in shame as the teachers scolded, reasoned, and tried to teach them; all at once.

'No T.V. for you all for a week, that will be your punishment', concluded Ma'am Dhoundiyal. 'Let's go, teachers.'

'And where are you two coming from?' Miss Tiwari asked Anjali and Arushi as they entered the classroom.

'We had gone to the washroom', Arushi replied quickly but there was an unmissable twinkle in her eyes. Miss Tiwari frowned at her, 'Is that all? You weren't up to any mischief?'

'No, ma'am', replied Anjali as Arushi turned to hide her smile.

The day was done!

THE REUNION

~ *Anurag Sinha*

Viresh nursed his coffee mug while skimming the newspaper in the morning sun. The coffee was roasted to perfection and brewed to his liking. His favourite jazz song lingered on the ears. It was a perfect Sunday!

"You and your dreadful jazz, why don't you ever play some *bhajans*?"

Ramya hollered from the kitchen.

"I am waiting for a phone call." Viresh retorted curtly, and then, added, "It's about the reunion, and please be soft. What will the neighbours think?"

He looked forward to the reunion of his school with earnestness. It offered a perfect opportunity to brag and network with other whiz kids. After all, he had earned his success. He was the vice president of a Fortune 500 company. His apartment was on a fashionable street in uptown Bangalore. He enjoyed a fat salary and missed out on little things in life.

Ramya maintained her sarcasm, "To hell with the neighbours. You and your middle-aged baldies are always anxious to relive their high school wet dreams while their wives wither away in household drudgery."

"What do you know about reunions, you have never been to one," muttered Viresh.

The phone call came as a relief. He picked up the phone and walked out of earshot. His high school chum, Sameer was on the line.

"Hey Bonky, have you firmed up your travel plans, this time it's a one-week affair."

"Samy amigo, everything is set and on schedule, who all are

joining from our batch?"

"Shaila will be there this time and so will be the other usual suspects."

Viresh's heart skipped a beat. Shaila was quite an opportunity, but he could never muster enough courage.

She was not a regular, but when she came, she set many a heart racing. During the last reunion's gala ball, Sameer and Shaila had danced with abandon. Viresh envied Sameer for that.

Sameer continued, "Do you recall Skimpy? He left school in the eighth class. He is coming too."

Viresh took a guess, "You mean that skinny Yogi, who threw the dorm bell in the khud and was rusticated for that."

"Atta boy!", quipped Sameer. "Skimpy too is based out of Bangalore. You can connect with him and travel together. He is there in our reunion group chat".

Viresh always dreaded the three-hour boring flight from

Bangalore to Dehradun. "Oh yes! A good company is not in harm's way."

It was time to reconnect with Yogi. He looked up Yogi's number and made the call.

"Hey Yogi! It's me, Viresh."

"Hey Viresh, how are you? I was expecting your call. Sameer had filled me in about you."

"That's great, I am good, how about you?'

" I am good. Why don't we catch-up over a drink?"

"Sure, shall we meet at The Oberoi, MG Road on coming Saturday, at about 7?"

"That's too snobby, why don't we meet at Pecos, it's got some local vibe, same time."

"Fine" replied Viresh and wondered, "Who rejects an invitation to a 5-star bar!"

On Saturday, at five to seven, Yogi walked in. Viresh took a mental note of Yogi's cotton kurta pajama, cheap sandals, and HMT Janata watch. "Who wears that!", not worth my time, he thought.

The reunion over drinks at Pecos was a short one and

uncharacteristic of two childhood chums meeting after a long time. Viresh thought of confessing that it was he who had snitched to the master on duty about the missing bell but decided against it.

On the D-day, he snored throughout the flight to Dehradun with Yogi sitting quietly beside him. The taxi laboured its way through the mountainous road, navigating many familiar bends and curves to reach the *The Queen of Hills*. Crisp mountain air welcomed their tired souls. The accommodation was pre-arranged by Sameer. His room had a dazzling view of Doon valley shimmering in the night light. He felt a rush of happiness and waited for his pals to join him for drinks.

At the reunion, there were the usual suspects from his batch. Shaila was there and so were many unfamiliar faces. Sameer occupied the center stage and was deft in the role of master of ceremonies.

He announced, "This is a very special reunion as we have in attendance for the very first time Mr. & Mrs. Yogi."
"Who is this mysterious Mrs. Yogi?," wondered Viresh.

To his surprise, the gathering parted for Shaila to join center-stage.

In a rare show of bonhomie and good humour, Shaila talked about Yogi's life as a writer and how he had supported her in her business venture, in both good and bad times.

Sameer then announced that Yogi has been nominated for the Booker prize and the alumni association is honouring him with the 'most distinguished alumnus award' in bringing glory to the school.

There was an air of expectancy for Yogi to join the center stage and reminisce about his school days.

The scene was rolling too fast for Viresh. Through the corner of his eyes, he saw Yogi gesturing to him to join the center stage. And then he heard him speak.

"My dearest friends, I recall one of my most memorable days in the school. It was a cold morning, the dormitory attendant rang the rising bell at sharp 6 AM. Viresh's bed was next to me and he had spent the previous night shivering under his blanket. The next morning, he overslept and received his first "rite of passage" by the matron. I saw the bearer, gleefully hovering over Viresh's misery. It was then that I decided to teach both of them, a lesson to remember!"

Yogi turned to Viresh and hugged him, his mouth now close to Viresh's ear. "I knew what you did. It's cool man. I did what I had to do." Viresh was quick in offering his apology.

Two friends separated once by the bell were now united.

———◆———

NOSTALGIA 1959

~ Vipin Sehgal

When I joined OG in 1959, in the 8th standard, the school was undergoing a painful transition to Indianisation under the strong and able leadership of Mr. Pasricha. The Senior Cambridge batch had, literally, God-like stalwarts such as School Captain Jag Mohan Verma, tall, strong, and dashing, ably supported by the likes of Bhanot, Somesh Bose, and the snake slaying Singh.

Led by Mr. Edwards, was a great team of teachers such as Messrs Ahmed, Banerjee, Chimwal, Dina, Fletcher, Gomes, Kelkar, Kukreti, and Luther.

Mr. Ahmed could never be interrupted from his teaching.

While lecturing in class one day, when he also happened to be the Master on Duty for the day, he had to step out into the corridor to investigate a disturbance. While walking down the corridor to the point of disturbance and back, Mr. Ahmed continued with his lecture uninterrupted, the textbook intact in his hand all this while, his voice resonating along the corridor loud and clear without missing a beat.

Mr. Ahmed also enticed many into reading newspapers by sharing with us titillating details of the Nanavati case unfolding in the Bombay courtrooms. I have been addicted to news papers since then to the eternal consternation of my better half and children. I passed the bug on by introducing Leslie Tocher to the Hindustan Times, this time bringing to his attention their carrying the Comic Strip Buck Ryan on Page 2. There was no stopping Leslie after that. He would charge out of the Dining Hall after lunch, beating everybody to the Library to get the first crack at the day's Hindustan Times.

Even in those innocent days, OG had its own peculiar denizens such as Garmi the friendly waiter, Jhuria the taciturn wake-upper and bed maker, and the Husky Bhotu, more Polar Bear than a dog, but gentle as a monk. Talking about monks, a high point of 1959 was the exile of Dalai Lama. The first place Nehru brought him to was Mussoorie, and I remember classes were canceled, and we were all sent down to Kulukhet to welcome him. Coincidentally, I ran into the Dalai Lama again in the late 1990s on the street in Toronto. Disgracefully the Canadian Government of the time (and even today), worried about offending China, refused to accord him official status, so he was reduced to walking along with a retinue of one, but that didn't dim his smile. I did mention to him about cheering him on at Kulukhet, and he was gracious enough to say he remembered, but I doubt it he did.

One other diversion, while on the subject of the Dalai Lama and Tibet - Carolyn Martin nee Fraser, an Old Oak Grovian, mentioned discovering in the Hospital Library the book on which the film Great Escape was based. I had a similar epiphany during the major Chicken Pox, Measles, and Mumps epidemics of 1961, when I scored the Trifecta of contracting all three in succession. During my stay, I came across and read Seven Years in Tibet, which was also later made into an atrocious film, starring Brad Pitt. What made reading the book so personal was the discovery that on his escape from Clement Town prison in Dehradun,

Heinrich Harrer actually went through the grounds of OG, on his escape to Tibet. The other warm memory from the stay in the hospital was a beautiful young nurse, among four brought in to cope with the number of kids in the hospital due to the epidemic. She was in love with me. Absolutely. No two ways about it. Every evening she brought me a toffee. If that doesn't convince you nothing will! She too went back to Delhi after the epidemic, taking my heart with her. Fortunately, I managed to retrieve it shortly thereafter, but that's another story.

Back to '59, we used to be woken up each morning by Jhuria clanging the large, heavy, hand-held bell, up and down the dormitory. Those of us who weren't affected by the bell, got a rude awakening courtesy Mr. Meston's cane on our nether parts. Once awoken thus, a quick wash-up was followed by two rounds, at least, of running around the back-pitch before breakfast. There was a 15-minute break before class, during which a student each from standards 9, 10, and 11 went to the Garden in front of the Headmaster's Office, opened the Meteorological Box, noted the High and Low temperatures, and measured overnight precipitation, all recorded in a Log Book. Mr. Fletcher reported these figures on a periodic basis to the appropriate Government of India authorities. I really regretted the dying down of this practice once he left to join Campion school in Bombay.

In those days, and I am sure even now, OG had its very own peculiar slang. My introduction to it was when I was standing around in class and Francis "Mule" (after "Francis the Talking Mule" Comics and Movies) Samuels, the prefect told me to "perch". It took me a while to figure out that I was being asked to sit down. Other examples are not for polite company, but are very funny. Even now when I explain some of these I have folks in stitches.

In classrooms, we used to have twinned desks. One bench occupied by two students, with a single top divided into two desktops. Each desktop was inclined, and hinged, covering a cavity for books and other study material. Each desktop was latched to enable locking. Invariably, keys would be lost and latches broken. The problem was solved by hammering nails into the inclined top, in the edge abutting the other top, so that when the other top came down, both desks would be locked when the other was.

Trouble was, this provided an opportunity for great mischief, to the guy with nails in his top. He could always disrupt you by insisting on opening his top while you were studying, so that you were forced to lift your top as well and could do nothing until he decided to close his lid. You get the picture. I remember this clearly, because K. K. Sabharwal, my desk mate, would do this to me very often. We got into a major disagreement, and he poked the back of my hand with the point of his compass. Infuriated, I let fly with my right hand holding a pencil. I hit him on the left side and ended up breaking the lead in his chest, drawing blood. He started to cry, and I started to sweat, as we were both convinced he was going to die. Needless to say, we both survived to tell the tale.

About this time we were introduced to Hydrogen Sulphide gas by Mr. Chimwal, in the Chemistry lab. Given the possibilities presented by its smell, I promptly purloined a few pellets of Ferrous Sulphide and poured some Hydrochloric acid in my Quink Ink bottle. The idea was to disrupt the after dinner study period. As providence would have it, Mr. Gomes, the best Math Teacher I ever had, was Master on Duty that night. Mr. Gomes had a unique way of wagging his index finger under his nostrils whenever he detected noxious smelling human emissions. Barely had I opened the bottle of acid and dropped in the

Ferrous Sulphide pellets that the chemical reaction started in full force. The concoction was bubbling and emitting the god awful smells sending Leroy D'Cunha, my new deskmate, into paroxysms of giggles, thus alerting Mr. Gomes, who came running. I quickly tried closing the bottle, but the telltale smell continued to hover around my desk. Mr. Gomes' index finger went into full wag mode, and the continuing chemical reaction sent the cap of the half-closed bottle flying. There was complete and utter pandemonium in the classroom. My classmates cried from laughing so hard. I single-handedly sent Tagore House down to first place in the ignominy department with the black marks I earned that night.

Phew, and that wasn't even all of '59! Those were the days.

HONOUR BOARD

Author	Oak Grove batch
Pat Corbett	1955
Vipin Sehgal	1963
Raghu Menon	1987
Anurag Sinha	1991
Manoj Panikkar	1991
Sweta Srivastava Vikram	1993
Amit Suri	1995
Gary Senger	1995
Mangu Srinivas	1995
Nitin Dubey	1995
Kanishka Mallick	1996
Sudip Bajpai	1996
Vikas Chandra	2003
Raveesh Gupta	2004
Nikhil Kumar	2005
Tabish Nawaz	2005
Priyanka Pandey	2005
Shrikant Avi	2006
Vani Raj	2012
Prabhat Ranjan	2018

ACKNOWLEDGEMENTS

Does the road wind up-hill all the way? Yes, to the very end.
~ Christina Rossetti

At the end is gratitude, love and respect for all of them
who made it happen.

Thank you Mr. Ganesh Saili for the lovely foreword.

Thank you Late Pat Corbett, Vipin Sehgal, Raghu
Menon, Anurag Sinha, Manoj Panikkar, Sweta
Srivastava Vikram, Amit Suri, Gary Senger, Mangu
Srinivas, Nitin Dubey, Kanishka Mallick, Sudip Bajpai,
Vikas Chandra, Raveesh Gupta, Nikhil Kumar, Tabish
Nawaz, Priyanka Pandey, Shrikant Avi, Vani Raj,
Prabhat Ranjan for your beautiful stories.

Thank you Nikhil Kumar, Puneet Monga, Manoj
Panikkar and Tabish Nawaz for your apt feedback and
incisive edits.

Thank you Sucharita Suri for the lovely illustration
and cover design.

Thank you Oakgrovians - students, staff, alumni - for
the amazing childhood and wonderful memories.

Thank you Oak Grove.

AFTERWORD

To live a childhood as a boarder in a residential school
is an experience that many of us have either lived or
contemplated about. Childhood is a phase of life when
we welcome the world with innocence and excitement, a
combination of which opens doors to wonders, to stories,
to friendships, and to life.

If you too grew up in a boarding school, and have stories
to share, then write to us. We can help you publish your
stories, or anthology of stories, of your lovely school.

TWAGAA INTERNATIONAL
https://twagaa.com
hello@twagaa.com

www.ingramcontent.com/pod-product-compliance
Lightning Source LLC
LaVergne TN
LVHW041517170726

843492LV00005B/1538

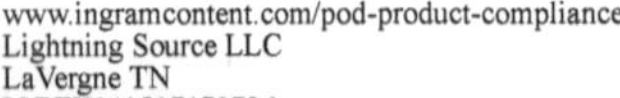